CW01594507

PEN

First Abolis

202 Arguments Against Economic Rationalism

Bob Ellis divides his time between screenwriting, film directing, broadcasting, song writing, acting, mob oratory, regular journalism and ceremonial speech writing, a rigorous round of dining out and theatre-going, and his family in Palm Beach, north of Sydney.

His screenwriting credits, *Newsfront, Goodbye Paradise, Maybe This Time* and the Paul Cox collaborations, *Man of Flowers* and *My First Wife*, all won major Australian prizes; as did his historical mini-series co-written with Stephen Ramsay, *True Believers*; his musical play, *The Legend of King O'Malley*, co-written with Michael Boddy; and his children's films, *Fatty Finn, Top Kid* and *The Paper Boy*. To this, he adds his three directorial feature films, *Unfinished Business, Warm Nights on a Slow Moving Train* and *The Nostradamus Kid*.

His political books, *The Things We did Last Summer, Two Weeks in Another Country, Letters to the Future* and *Goodbye Jerusalem*, his collection of *The Inessential Ellis* and his comic novel, *The Hewson Tapes*, are regarded in his native land as small classics. His position as a war correspondent, social commentator, theatre owner, documentary director, dispirited collaborator with Werner Hertzog, nightclub turn and political mover is possibly unique.

Bob Ellis' hobbies are eating, conversation, film going, cricket, reading and exploring the Ring of Kerry. He is now in his fifties, overweight but healthy, and a curiously happy man.

BOB ELLIS

First Abolish the Customer

202 Arguments Against Economic Rationalism

PENGUIN BOOKS

Penguin Books Australia Ltd
487 Maroondah Highway, PO Box 257
Ringwood, Victoria 3134, Australia
Penguin Books Ltd
Harmondsworth, Middlesex, England
Penguin Putnam Inc.
375 Hudson Street, New York, New York 10014, USA
Penguin Books Canada Limited
10 Alcorn Avenue, Toronto, Ontario, Canada M4V 3B2
Penguin Books (NZ) Ltd
Cnr Rosedale and Airborne Roads, Albany, Auckland, New Zealand
Penguin Books (South Africa) (Pty) Ltd
4 Pallinghurst Road, Parktown 2193, South Africa

First published by Penguin Books Australia 1998

1 2 3 4 5 6 7 8 9 10

Copyright © Bob Ellis 1998

All rights reserved. Without limiting the rights under copyright reserved above, no part of this publication may be reproduced, stored in or introduced into a retrieval system, or transmitted, in any form or by any means (electronic, mechanical, photocopying, recording or otherwise), without the prior written permission of both the copyright owner and the above publisher of this book.

Cover design by Guy Mirabella and Leonie Stott, Penguin Design Group
Typeset in New Baskerville by Post Pre-press Group
Printed in Australia by Australian Print Group, Maryborough, Victoria

National Library of Australia
Cataloguing-in-Publication data:

Ellis, Bob.
First abolish the customer: 202 arguments against economic rationalism.

ISBN 0 14 028123 1.

1. Economics – Australia. 2. Australia – Economic policy – 20th century.
I. Title.

338.994

This book is dedicated to my mother
Elsie Lillian Ward Ellis
who in eighty-seven years has seen
many economic certitudes,
and survived them all.

The author acknowledges the aid and encouragement given him by Winton Higgins, Associate Professor of Politics, specialising in Political Economy at Macquarie University, Sydney, Australia, the work of John Ralston Saul, John Maynard Keynes, Nugget Coombs, Neville Wran, Gore Vidal, Nick Rowley, Will Hutton, Ben Chifley, Kim Beazley, Don Dunstan, Mike Rann, Mike Moore, Mick Dodson, Syd Hickman, John Clarke, Al Capp, Stephen Sondheim, Patrick Cook and Joseph Heller, and the many, many radio reports and searching interviews of the Australian Broadcasting Corporation in the nineteen eighties and nineties.

To begin, as the dead poet said,
at the beginning.

1

Economic rationalism at its heart is a refusal to spend money on the unnecessary. If a company can make a bigger profit by shedding this or that worker, it should do so. This is regardless of how much the worker has done for the company in the past, or for how long he has done it, or whether he has worked well or loyally or selflessly. If he is now superfluous to company needs, or a drain on company profits, or a threat to the overall profit level of company shareholders – if he is, in short, no longer *worth his hire* – he should go, however untidily, and seek work elsewhere or go on the dole.

This attitude is not too hard to understand given human tendencies of the past five thousand years.

What is remarkable is the belief – a belief all economic rationalists publicly share – that this decisive, sudden process of sacking people is good for society, or good for the economy as a whole.

By sacking people in their hundreds of thousands, the theory at its heart asserts, you *create* employment and stimulate spending.

A moron could see the opposite is true. But not an economic rationalist.

2

For a man out of a job is a man with little money to spend on anything but food and bus fares to his next job interview. He has no spare cash for shirts or shoes or handkerchiefs or cars or house extensions or videotape hire or sandstone for his planned wine cellar or new skis. His sacking has ended his ability to do anything much that is of use to an expanding economy.

3

It has ended as well his wife's capacity to spend money. If she has a job herself she is with difficulty supporting him and the children, and scraping to pay the rent or keep up the mortgage, or bitterly arguing against the advice of moneylenders that they forthwith sell the house.

4

It has ended moreover his *children's* capacity to spend money – on toys or CDs or skateboards or video games or Big Macs or nights at the cinema seeing *Titanic* or James Bond.

Every man sacked, in short, stops four people – four people at least – from spending money on things other than basic food and basic shelter, and bus transport to the next job interview.

5

When, as happened last year in Canberra, Australia, thirty thousand public servants are sacked by a government keen on cutting costs and saving the taxpayers' money, one hundred and twenty thousand people – one hundred and twenty thousand people at least – ceased spending money meaningfully in Canberra.

This put pressure on many Canberra small businesses. Many of these responded to the pressure by sacking people. Others responded by closing up shop and putting their family home on the market. These family homes were competing with the abandoned family homes of the sacked public servants, and Canberra house prices therefore dramatically dropped. This rational market response further pressured the families of the sacked workers and heightened their despair.

Some of them sought relief in drugs or alcohol. Some of them took up burglary to fund their new lifestyles. Some of them committed suicide. Some of them blundered onward in their limited lives, sought work, lost it, got drunk a lot and beat their wives. A lot of grief was caused, and a good few years spent in gaol. And the increase in crime put up insurance premiums.

And the Prime Minister called this process rational. And the Prime Minister is an honourable man.

6

Economic rationalism is a process that can be summed up, pretty well, in the following slogan: First Abolish the Customer.

Hold onto that thought. And follow the thread.

7

It might be interesting, I think, to apply this theory of rationalism to the way we conduct ourselves in other fields, and see how truly rational it seems.

It is not economically rational, for instance, to buy books, especially books you will probably read only once and put aside, when by waiting a little you can borrow almost any book you want from the library and not pay for it, or not pay much. If you were a true economic rationalist you would never buy another book.

But . . . if everybody did this, if nobody bought books anymore, if everybody applied the rules of economic rationalism to the common pastime of reading books, if everybody like good rationalists avoided expenditure on the unnecessary, then sooner or later the writing of books would cease, and the publication of books would cease, because there would be no money in it. Printeries worldwide would go bust, or transfer their efforts to Christmas cards. And nearly all book publishers, except those supplying how-to guides for machinery. And nearly all publisher's readers and publisher's editors, and book reviewers in the newspapers, and the editors of book pages and literary magazines. And bookshops would close, and the people who work in them – young college graduates and delicate old chain-smoking women – would be sooner or later all of them out of work.

And authors too. They would need to find something else to do with their lives, in some other sector of the workforce. Reciting poetry, perhaps, in front of an upturned hat on a wintry street.

If everybody gave up buying books, in short, an economically rational thing to do, a fair number of people, maybe twenty or twenty-five thousand in Australia – 0.2 percent of the workforce – would be put out of work. Four hundred thousand people in the United States.

And less reading would be done overall. And fewer things learned. And fewer things found out by writers and passed on. And fewer discoveries made.

So what is economically rational for the individual is, *in this case*, economically hurtful to the nation, and probably the world.

This pattern, of the squeeze in one place that then hurts everywhere, is what follows on from economic rationalism almost everywhere.

8

Because the cutting of the costs of an individual enterprise is not all that happens. For that cost-cutting does things to the people who are cut with the cost. And they do things in response, not always predictable things. In the same way that it is not easy to predict from the first loud scattering of pool balls on a green felt table where the orange-striped ball will be eighteen shots from now, it is not always easy to guess what a nation's economy will be doing nine months from now, nine months after a public authority, say, is triumphantly privatised, or a dollar floated, or an interest rate brought down to five percent, or up to eight percent, or a gambling casino licensed to grab the spare cash of the lower classes.

It depends a lot on what the economy's customers do, and customers are people, with sometimes unpredictable responses. The invention of radio did not wipe out the gramophone, for instance, nor the invention of television the radio, nor the cinema the live theatre, nor colour television the cinema, though all these things were loudly proclaimed extinct in their decades of challenge by people expert in their field. What should be logical when you look at the figures is, *because people are human*, hardly ever so.

9

'Economies exist,' Robert Bolt said, 'because people trade, and not the other way around.' And why people trade, or refuse to buy new products (the Edsel motor car, the Betamax video recorder, the television telephone, the movie of *Evita* starring Madonna) is sometimes a mystery.

Hold onto that thought.

10

Because it shouldn't be too difficult, for instance, using rationalist logic, to persuade people to stop wasting money on contraceptives and spend the fifteen or so extra dollars a week on real estate, or the currency market, or building a concrete carpark, or other profit-rich investments.

Contraceptives, it can be plausibly argued, are unnecessary when the alternatives of oral sex or coitus interruptus are easy to learn and free of charge. All that is required, as in all economic rationalism, is a change of *attitude* in the participants, an exercise of *discipline.*

But . . . if everybody took this advice and ceased buying contraceptives, there would soon be no more contraceptives manufactured because there would be no money in it. And many young people now at work in the rubber plantations of Malaysia would be quickly unemployed, and many more young people now at work in the factories that make the Pill. And gynaecologists at present advising their women patients on oestrogen levels would make less money, and employ fewer staff, and so, in due course, would the chemists who sell them.

And hundreds of thousands of people across the world would be out of work, and miserably retraining for other jobs. Millions, perhaps.

And there would be (of course) more accidental pregnancies, and more abortions, and because of these abortions more eventual miscarriages, and because of these miscarriages more childless women undergoing depression in psychiatric wards at the taxpayers' expense, and a rise in taxes to pay for them.

And more illegitimate births, and more adoptions, and more regretted adoptions ending up in custody disputes between natural mothers and foster parents, and more torn miserable children going crazy in their teens and early twenties and suiciding in gaol.

More sadness, in short, all round. And all because of a typical shortsighted rationalist calculation aimed at saving fifteen dollars a week.

It would be better, on the whole, to *spend* the fifteen dollars.

11

Keep always in mind that no academic rationalist practises what he preaches. If he did, he would take no wages from his university or his thankful corporation, and merely give lectures for which the public would buy tickets to attend – or not buy tickets to attend. He would subject himself to market forces, and, if his lectures were boring, go broke.

But he will never do this. No way. He prefers the protection of the institution he works for, and the regular wages it pays him, to the rough rude winds of cruel and random chance.

In this regard, and only this regard, he is very like the rest of us – an armchair traveller on the tossing seas of commerce, a phantom buccaneer on the high seas of market risk, safe in his bed, and on his comfortable university salary, every night.

12

As a matter of interest, there has only been one economic theoretician, or only one famous one, who has made money in great amounts by investing it wisely. He did it for his Alma Mater, Kings College, of Cambridge.

His name was John Maynard Keynes.

13

Lord Keynes was the most influential economist of the thirties, forties, fifties, sixties and seventies, revered alike by Roosevelt, Attlee, Menzies, Churchill, J.K. Galbraith and Nugget Coombs. He believed that governments must interfere in the economy when interference is appropriate – in time of war, for instance, or deep recession – and when interference is inappropriate, not interfere at all.

He believed that jobs must be created, however useless (like park-maintenance youth corps, or local theatre groups, or acting schools, or the study of insect migrations), be *invented*, if need be, when the alternative is criminal chaos, widespread starvation, the destruction of local communities and the threat of revolution. He believed (and Roosevelt, following his lead, likewise believed) that a certain level of sustainable debt, and a certain level of unavoidable inflation, were a small price to pay for political tranquillity and the chance for all to prosper and die happy.

14

'In the long run,' he famously said, 'we are all dead.'

15

This means the solutions must be *now*, or soon, and not fifty years down the track. Keynes loathed the economic chaos imposed on Germany by the treaty that ended World War I and masterminded in 1944 the Bretton Woods Agreement that ensured the economic recovery of Germany and Europe and made possible the welfare state that Britain enjoyed under

Attlee, Churchill, Eden, Macmillan, Home and Wilson; a golden age of equal opportunity where, for a time, class barriers did not altogether stifle the talent of the less well born; an age of liberated calm and creativity, and a humane society at peace.

16

Lord Keynes is now regarded by the economic rationalists as a dangerous lunatic. They have better solutions in mind.

17

Economic rationalists believe that the market, however skittish, should be allowed to do what it likes, whatever the human cost, and shareholders' whims must override civilised values whenever the two are in conflict.

That towns, whole towns, like Newcastle or Leeton and much of the north of England and much of Wales, must be sacrificed when the price is right.

And the price is right when a profit in billions is made for the shareholders and the board of directors by the company selling up, closing down and moving on.

Hold onto that thought.

And follow the thread.

18

It is not economically rational either, when you come to think of it, to keep a dog, for the money spent on Towser and his food and grooming and worming could go into cane-toad futures or the bullion market. (A cat is a different matter because it keeps down rats and noisy roving native animals that with their shrieks and scutterings keep the economically efficient householder frantically awake at night and render him insufficiently attentive to the nuances of early morning phone calls from the New York head office). Dogs, by rationalist logic, must go. They cost too much, and do not, in an age of video surveillance, anymore earn their keep.

Never mind that dogs keep many old women sane (dogs are the worst paid psychoanalysts of our time, discuss) and prepare young children and teenagers for the challenges and compromises of parenthood. A dog's figures do not add up.

Get rid of Towser: he is expendable. Do it now.

19

It can be likewise argued, using this mindset, that it isn't economically rational to spend money on Christmas holidays in the family shack by the beach, when the two or two and a half thousand dollars spent there might be invested in gold futures or property development or shares in Camel cigarettes. Christmas holidays, it can be argued, take up fourteen or twenty-one days when the vigilant investor might use that time cleaning up on the falling yen or the rising Eurodollar. And if he *sold* the beachside shack for two hundred thousand dollars he could be cleaning up with the added investment cash flow, cleaning up very big.

Christmas holidays are anyway a drag, requiring you to dissemble fervently to a wildly varying group of people you would mostly avoid if they were strangers, and the myth of Christmas is positively harmful because it suggests that things you wish for will come your way because you infantilely beseech a white-bearded, roving deity whipping reindeers through the night sky to give them to you – when in fact they come, if they do at all, as a result of long hours over the computer terminal, crunching the figures and playing the odds.

But . . . a loss of that Christmas experience, that mingling of the generations, means that children go out into the world less prepared for human unexpectedness and personal adversity, and can therefore end up on drugs and prove an expense to their parents. It can mean precious family knowledge is not passed on, nor family traditions revered, and the pride in a family name that goes down further generations is never enhanced. It can mean the gentle experience of human kindness and gratitude and grandparental affection round the Christmas tree is never experienced, and a cold view of the human condition is therefore emphasised in the mind of children who eventually, therefore, sometimes suicide. It can breed an attitude that fills the nation's prisons with young men sure that society is unkind and unjust. And the cost of new prisons can put up income taxes to a degree that is greater than the amount of money saved by not having Christmas at all.

And Christmas, too, though costly to the individual, is good for the economy – for beach towns and theme parks and family restaurants and boat-hiring and scuba-diving small businesses, for toy manufacturers and motel owners and video-renting small businessmen and the young assistants who work for them, and the young people starting out at McDonald's and Kentucky Fried Chicken and Woolworths on their holidays.

And though it began as an arguable myth and a dodgy proposition – that Jeshua Ben Yusef was born of a virgin the proper King of Israel through the descent line of his *father* and He will return soon in a bright cloud with a sharp sickle to save the righteous of humankind from the Devil's clutches – Christmas has its uses.

It may be only a dream, but good solid things can come from it, and great good on earth.

Hold onto that thought.

20

Economic rationalism bizarrely believes (and this is not a joke) that the market knows what it's doing.

This means that if a business or a corporation or a country goes bust it deserves to go bust, because it wasn't behaving efficiently or competitively. That if a new soft-drink company is out-advertised by Coca Cola and so goes bust, this is what that soft-drink company deserved. That if an animation company is outgunned by Disney and so doesn't get the cinema distribution it needs to make its money back, this is what it deserved. That if Ireland after eight hundred years of English occupation, murder, land theft, religious persecution, hanging, torture, starvation and intermittent civil slaughter has a weakened economy and an insufficient industrial base or a poor business attitude or an over-developed liking for Guinness, it's all Ireland's fault, and Ireland asking for special treatment from England and reparation for past wrongs is a really odious form of whingeing. That if your particular cultural habit is not to behave in the usual American cut-throat, hit-and-run, cannibalise-and-move-on capitalist way, you deserve to stew, you poor sad fool, in your own juice.

Because the market is wise and it knows what it's doing. The market, in fact, is the only available wisdom there is. The market is the only arbiter, the only divinity, that can be trusted.

So when the market decides to pay, for instance, eight hundred thousand dollars for a furtively accomplished snapshot of someone sucking Fergie's big toe the market is behaving rationally. That if the market offers fifteen million dollars for an interview with O.J. Simpson because it thinks he might be a murderer, it is behaving with economic wisdom. That a book of black-and-white pictures of Madonna swinging naked over a crowded street is worth more, in market terms, than a book of paintings by Degas, and well worth the money at twice the price.

And when it closed down two hundred Welsh and Scottish and English coal mines that were still making money – not much, but making a profit – and forced their once proud citizens into freezing beggary in cardboard boxes on the streets of London and Birmingham, it had achieved the best possible outcome in the present economic cycle. When, after closing down coal mines, it continued to make *land* mines and sell them in Africa and Asia, where they blew little children's arms and legs off, it was reacting to market pressures with wisdom.

Land mines, not coal mines.

Land mines make more money.

21

It also means that if your house burns down in a bushfire set by a firebug you are only getting what you deserve.

Of course you are.

You should have behaved more efficiently, by living in a society without firebugs, or trees, or summer heat.

You got what you deserved.

22

The Australian resort town of Thredbo got what it deserved too when a landslide one midnight plunged a chalet into a ravine and eighteen people under the freezing rubble took hours to die and one man, Stuart Diver, five days to be dug out, after which, and after the national prayers of thanks, he was given a job as a TV announcer on four hundred thousand dollars a year, and began to smile again.

In its wisdom, it seemed, the market had decided that a ski resort be built in Thredbo in the 1950s. The market then decided – robustly, against the advice of interfering bureaucrats – to build a row of chalets on an unsafe, unstable steep hillside. The market then allowed the chalet owners to make money for forty years. The market then decided to bring the whole hill down – in chaos, ruin and slaughter – and wreck the tourist potential of Thredbo perhaps forever.

The market wisely decided not only to extinguish eighteen people, but to give to Stuart Diver, the sole survivor – a happy, memorable rhyme – a bag of money for his good fortune. The taciturn heroes who dug him out, of course, will get nothing, and will lose their jobs and incomes, most of them, when the ski resort goes bust. The families of the dead victims will get no great reward either. The dead victims, in market parlance, did not shape up. They did not survive and become celebrities on television like Stuart, and the market decided they were expendable. They, and their families, got what they deserved.

The market has decided.

23

It is an odd thing, this belief that the market is a person, or a deity, or a godlike computer dispensing perfect justice, always oiled and smooth and balanced, never in need of repair. That the market is always in the know.

Not that it's a wayward force like the weather, against which you must arm yourself with umbrellas and raincoats and roofs and stone walls and sandbag levies by flood-prone rivers. But that it's an irresistible force, and so must not be resisted.

We are meant to suppose that this is a branch of *logic*, but it is, of course, a branch of religion. It is not far from the familiar funeral utterance, 'God moves in mysterious ways', and we are unwise to question His ways and His decisions which are always for the best. It is not far, indeed, from the Cargo Cults of recent times in the islands of the South Pacific, which held to the belief that by digging rudimentary air strips on your island you could tempt the magic aeroplanes to return, aeroplanes full of refrigerators and radios and gramophones, all the treasures of the gods – the gods that came here during World War II and then mysteriously went away.

Economic rationalists believe that magic will come back to society if you do a few simple things, wrecking the lives of everybody whose throat you can get your hands on and selling up machinery for scrap.

This will ensure the return, the theory says, of the mysterious magical refrigerators of yore.

24

This simple, simplistic, punishing puritan belief (if it is a belief, and not a deft camouflage for simple greed) is a product of America, of course. America has these crazes from time to time, and her economy runs on them until the market decides it is time for another craze.

25

One craze held that you must not drink alcohol anymore, so its production went underground, where many family fortunes – the Kennedys', for instance – were made between the flying bullets of Capone and Elliott Ness.

26

Another craze put forth, and successfully sold, the dizzying belief that Soviet Russia, which had just seen twenty million of its people killed in a catastrophic war – the worst in its history – was now improbably determined to atomic bomb, invade and enslave America, and burn down all its churches, whatever the cost. And the only way for the Land of the Free to meet this imminent emergency was by building bombs and rocket launchers and tanks and aircraft carriers and digging fallout shelters and putting former communists in gaol. A lot of money, thousands of billions of dollars, was made by shareholders of companies using government contracts to build weapons that were never used, and couldn't be because they were so quickly obsolescent.

This fantasy became the basis of the American economy for forty years. Rockets and bombs were made while schools ran down and slums grew into maggot heaps of crime and the prison population rose to two million, the highest in the world, eighty percent of it black Americans. It was an economy built on a fantasy of imminent all-out war with godless barbarians.

The Soviet Union never planned to invade and subjugate America. It was hard enough keeping in line its border states of Poland and Hungary and Czechoslovakia and rebuilding brick by brick – and heroic statue by statue – its own devastated great cities.

But it did react to America's bombs and rockets by building – defensively, always defensively – bombs and rockets, and eventually space rockets, of its own with money it, too, could have spent on worthier things.

A fantasy, then, fathered much of the world economy in the nineteen fifties, sixties and seventies.

Fantasies can do that.

Fantasies like economic rationalism.

Less and less flesh

27

If economic rationalism, the theory, is not just a fig leaf for the old Adam of market greed, the greed that talks up prices, sells fast and moves on – and we must entertain this as a possibility – then it can only be a kind of punishing neurosis, unlinked with market logic.

A similar neurosis exists, in fact, which has been widely studied by psychopathologists.

It is called anorexia.

28

Anorexia is a belief by the sufferer that less and less flesh on bones is the only road to beauty and success. The sufferer, usually a teenage girl, eats less and less and convinces herself that her image in the mirror is comelier and comelier as her body weight contracts, her bones stick out, her menstrual cycle ceases, and extensive kidney and liver damage begins to threaten her life.

If accused of having the disease she will often deny it, and plead another disease, and often pretend to eat, or eat and throw up afterwards. Pretty soon she is living in a fantasy and telling lies to anyone concerned at her condition, lying to doctors and stealing from parents and friends and relatives, going missing and starving on the run, pursuing like a drug addict the single sustaining fantasy that will slowly, or not so slowly, extinguish her life. Less and less flesh on bones, her motto would seem to be, till only dead bones are left.

29

Economic rationalism likewise believes in less and less flesh on bones till only dead bones are left. It believes that a company can be dieted and starved into leanness and meanness, efficiency and therefore success, that slim is beautiful and famine profitable. A company may have three tiers of middle management, and two of these are removed. It may have a PR department that goes, a mail office that goes, an apprenticeship-training section that goes, a tea lady who is retrenched, a food trolley cancelled. It may sell off one of its three buildings. And it may then post a profit for that year, and the following year, that is twenty-two percent higher than it was.

It has looked in the mirror, and found beauty there.

But . . . then, of course, its board of directors, inflamed with the taste of fresh profits, demands further economies, and the liver-killing phase of the anorexia begins.

Spare parts are no longer made in-house, but bought cheaply overseas, from companies equally fond of cheapness. Some of the spare parts are faulty, and, if the company is an airline, planes begin to crash, and the resultant scandal sends the company bankrupt. Or, less dramatically, if the company makes radios, the knobs fall off, or the tuning jams, and once loyal customers turn to another brand, and the company starts posting a loss and is sold off, usually to a multinational that sacks its management and many of its fearful remaining staff and absorbs it into its larger operation.

Its retrenched middle management, meanwhile, has held some meetings and started up a rival company of its own, using the expertise that is not counted as worthwhile property in the larger calculation, and this company, familiar with the local market, starts to make a dent in the customer base.

And the story continues.

30

An example of economic anorexia perhaps – and it could be called economic leprosy – is Australia's Telstra, the government-owned monopoly telephone company. The economic rationalist Howard government determined that it should be privatised, a somewhat unpopular move politically. So they decided, after taking soundings, that what they should do was privatise only a third of it and leave the rest, for the moment, in public hands, to pacify those customers insecure about their future as phone users and phone-bill payers.

But . . . in order to sell it off at the highest price, the government had to make it more efficient and competitive. Lean and mean. Anorexic.

They sacked and computerised and bought satellites, only one of which crashed to earth, and hired sharp, sadistic American cost-cutters and retrenchers, and pretty soon they'd posted an annual profit of 1.6 billion dollars.

'More,' said this anorexic board of directors, in this case the government.

So they sacked twenty-five thousand employees.

Many of these were from country towns. And these country towns as a result were severely damaged economically.

But the profit margin went up, and when the company was privatised the share price was huge, and the government made lots of money that it then could throw round its marginal seats and it was very happy with the outcome.

But . . . a great number of the sacked workers were telephone repairmen, and no-one was able to get their phones repaired easily anymore, or even installed, and up and down the main streets and the main roads of the country regions were public telephones that weren't working.

And people stopped using Telstra because there was a rival company, Optus, now allowed in the marketplace for economic rationalist reasons, which started picking up customers . . . And the story continues.

And the government found that their former customers, enraged at the fact that to merely make a call on a phone that worked was becoming a matter of unutterable complexity, began to tell pollsters they would vote the government out.

Thus economic anorexia achieved, as it always does, what anorexia mostly does, which is death to the true believer.

Less and less flesh on bones, till only dead bones are left.

31

There are other examples, probably, of this. BHP which announced it would sell its Newcastle Steelworks, thus gravely wounding that beautiful city's economy, and found, mysteriously, a record loss of 1.5 billion dollars the following year, and nationwide calls for the sacking of the geniuses that thought of it. The Australian universities, impoverished overnight by the Howard government, cut back staff and courses and put up fees to (sometimes) two hundred thousand dollars per degree, payable upfront, and then found, to their astonishment, Asian students going instead to Hawaii and New Zealand and Siberia, or gloomily refusing education altogether. The Victorian ambulance services, commanded by Premier Kennett to cost less and less, cut back on drivers and helicopters and found patients therefore plaintively waiting for hours and then dying, and scandal engulfing, accusing and punishing its bureaucracy for its part in what looked like murder.

Less and less flesh on bones, till only dead bones are left.

Hold onto that thought.

32

And so it is believed, or was at the time of writing. This bitter, punishing process of diet, starve and conquer is inevitable, it is believed, and to it there is no alternative. Because it's a global economy now, and we must be part of it. To be part of it we must compete.

To compete with slaves we must become slaves ourselves, or something very close to slaves.

It stands to reason. There is no alternative.

And yet there is, amazingly, a highly visible alternative, a place and a process that is in every way the opposite of this self-cannibalising process; an example, famous and vivid and widely praised, of economic gluttony; an example of large and constant profits in the international marketplace achieved through conspicuous waste.

It's called Hollywood.

33

A Hollywood that followed economic rationalist theory would be startlingly different from the Hollywood we know.

Costs would be coming down. Surplus personnel, like Associate Producers and Executive Producers and Co-producers and Agents and Clapper Boys and Stunt Doubles and Personal Assistants and Personal Hairdressers and Cockroach Wranglers would be daily accepting redundancy. Only the cheaper actors would be employed. The budgets of all movies made would be as they are in New Zealand – around eight hundred thousand dollars – in order to compete with New Zealand. There would be an emphasis on films shot quickly, in three or four weeks, films with no more than six or seven characters in them – like, say, *Sex Lies and Videotape* – and four or five locations, with cheap yet competent actors, working overtime unpaid. There would be no Hollywood star system. Actors would be paid what they get in the theatre – four hundred dollars or so a week. It would be economically irrational to pay them any more.

There would be no films like *Titanic.*

That would be a recipe for disaster.

34

Hollywood, however, did once go through a period of economic rationalism – in, of course, the 1980s.

In the 1980s Hollywood movies got shorter and shorter.

The reasoning behind this was to do with ticket sales and popcorn.

If movies were shorter, it was logically argued, there would be more sessions a day, and more popcorn sold between sessions.

Popcorn, it was reasoned, and soft drinks and chocolate icecreams, was where the cinema made its money. Movies were no more than the bait that drew the customer to his true destination, the popcorn counter, where he spent the bulk of his money.

So the time you spent in the cinema got less and less – from three and a half hours in the fifties when the programme was always either a double feature plus cartoons and newsreels, or a big blockbuster like *Ben Hur* or *Spartacus* or *Lawrence of Arabia*, to two and a quarter hours in the early seventies when there was a feature plus cartoons and shorts, to two hours in the late seventies when there was a feature plus trailers, to one and three quarter hours in the eighties when the movies, following rationalist logic, became ninety-five, then ninety, then eighty-five, then eighty, then seventy-five minutes. These included *Flashdance*, *Rocky III* and *Police Academy 3*, and their brevity meant a single cinema could have seven sessions a day, and eight opportunities to sell popcorn.

Curiously, though, the audiences stopped coming.

Being economic rationalists themselves, they believed they weren't getting their money's worth.

35

A night out at the movies, they argued, cost a lot of money. You bought petrol to get there. You spent money on the carpark, on the restaurant meal for yourself and perhaps your family before you went to the cinema, on babysitters if you went out as a couple, on popcorn and chocolates before and soft drinks after.

You therefore wanted your money's worth, and seventy-eight minutes – even of Sylvester Stallone getting his head punched in – felt more like being cheated. So no matter how many sessions there were every day, people weren't coming to any of them.

So overnight, in the early nineties, the time you spent in the cinema went up again, to two hours, two and a half hours, two hours forty. Even children's films, like *Hook*, were well over two hours in length.

Then, against all the tenets of both Hollywood and conventional wisdom and economic rationalism, somebody made *Titanic.*

36

Titanic had everything going against it. The hero died, and the villain survived. The story involved a series of flashbacks, and flashbacks (it was well known) were confusing and no current audience (it was well known) liked them. It was set in the past, and all big money-making films were set in the future, or the exciting, violent, metropolitan present. It had no big-name star, no Redford or Nicholson or Streisand or Schwarzenegger. It was a downer, possibly the ultimate downer. It took place mostly indoors. It involved ice and cold and freezing, which never, it was known, made money.

It was three and a quarter hours long.

That meant only three sessions a day.

And it cost a hundred million dollars.

Then, after reshoots and further stunt and model work, *two* hundred million dollars.

Titanic was economically irrational.

It had to fail.

37

Titanic sold more tickets and in real terms made more money than any film since *Gone With the Wind*. Its very extravagance became its prime attraction – extravagant costumes, an ongoing climax that in itself lasted over an hour.

Because extravagance, when you get down to really thinking about it, is often *in itself* an engine of earthly success, and a conspicuous waste of money, paradoxically, a way of making buckets of money.

This is not economically rational. But it's true.

38

That extravagance is often the father of money is a fact that has been long known. In ancient times the Seven Wonders of the World – each one a gargantuan extravagance – lured tourists in tens of thousands over perilous seas to gawp and wonder and buy souvenirs, to take ferry rides between the legs of the Colossus of Rhodes, or camel rides to the Pyramids, and guided tours through the Hanging Gardens of Babylon, and eat in the cafes afterwards, and thus increase the gross income of the adjacent cities and gratify their tax gatherers and enrich their tempestuous monarchs. Extravagance begot income, and royal wealth, in greater abundance than the original waste of money.

In the medieval world the Taj Mahal and Chartres Cathedral and the onion-shaped Church of St Basil in what is now Red Square and the Bayeux Tapestry and the Piazza del San Marco and Westminster Abbey did likewise; and in the modern world the Statue of Liberty, the Eiffel Tower, the Empire State Building, the faces on Mount Rushmore, the Sydney

Opera House and the whole great city of St Petersburg – extravagances cursed in their day as reprehensible waste by the emotional forefathers of economic rationalism.

Today in many small towns are the Big Bananas, Big Pineapples, Big Merinos and representations of Ayers Rock that continue to demonstrate the attractiveness of big spending and pointless extravagance.

As does, of course, the Sistine Chapel.

39

The Sistine Chapel was a project of Pope Julius II who proposed that Michelangelo paint on its extensive ceiling a copious dramatisation of the Creation, Fall and Salvation of Man.

Michelangelo began with reluctance, suffered backaches, drips of paint in the eyes and the chronic ailment of all good artists, procrastination.

'When will there be an end?' cried Pope Julius from the floor, far below.

'When it is finished,' growled Michelangelo.

Soon he was a year over the deadline, though 'soon' is perhaps not the word, and Pope Julius began to climb the scaffolding and hit at him with a stick.

It took two years longer than planned and in terms of the Vatican coffers was a financial catastrophe.

But. . . in the four hundred and fifty-six years since its completion the majestic awe-inspiring result, regarded widely now as the greatest work of art on the planet, has immeasurably enriched with the dollars of admiring tourists the exchequers of not only Italy but also the Catholic Church worldwide.

It went over budget, but it didn't matter. It proved, over time, a financial success.

And success is too small a word for what it eventually became, however momentarily financially embarrassing it proved in the long years between its genesis and its revelation.

It is a reason, in itself, to go to Italy. It is an example, in itself, of the opulent genius of that great culture. It is one of the reasons Italian film directors (for instance) are as a bunch the best and most confident in the history of the cinema. They stand on the shoulders of this giant work, and they can see forever.

40

An economic rationalist, however, would have sacked Michelangelo in the fourth year of his procrastination, on the same good and solid financial grounds as a later economic rationalist, one Davis Hughes (mentioned here for perhaps the last time in human history) who, having noted that the Sydney Opera House was already two years beyond its deadline and a thousand percent beyond its budget of a mere seven million pounds, sacked Joern Utzon, its architect, and drove him out of Australia, to which he never returned, and hired an architectural hack named Peter Hall (mentioned here for the last time in human history) to 'complete' it within a budget and within a time frame that made two of its performance spaces comfortless for actors and stage workers and sometimes inaudible for audiences, and save a few million pounds.

Had Pope Julius been of a similar dwarfish cast of mind he would have sacked Michelangelo and hired a hack church painter to 'complete' the mighty mural by a particular date and incur no more expenditure than a particular amount.

41

He would likewise, had he been a Hollywood producer, have sacked Charlie Chaplin, who took four years to make *The Great Dictator*, a work still showing and making money, and ordered it finished by a hack director willing to reduce its anti-Nazi message and thus pacify its potential exhibitors in Greater Nazi Germany.

42

He would have sacked Orson Welles from *The Magnificent Ambersons*, hailed by the few who saw it as better than *Citizen Kane*, and removed fifty minutes from its length, despite test screenings where the audience loved it, and so ruined it, and also ruined Welles.

And so he did. For this is what happened.

43

He would moreover have asked J.R.R. Tolkien to cut *The Lord of the Rings* to one third its length because there was a paper shortage in Britain and paper was dearer than usual, and it was not economically rational to publish a work of children's fiction at that length.

And so he did. For this happened too.

And J.R.R. Tolkien, thank heaven, told him to go to blazes.

And the book, at its original length, is still selling.

44

So the economic argument when applied to works of art is provably nonsense.

'I never heard a guy,' Billy Wilder once remarked, 'who said to me, "I've got to see this movie. I hear it came in under budget."'

45

Economies exist because people trade, and not the other way round.

Hold onto that thought.

And follow the thread.

46

Margaret Thatcher pursued economic rationalism with the zeal of Torquemada for eleven years, and her successor John Major even more ferociously for another seven. Electricity was privatised, rail lines cut back, free health services run down, state schools impoverished, Oxford and Cambridge asked to find more money in the private sector, the great theatre companies 'encouraged' to cut back, sack actors, avoid new works, tour overseas and put on American musicals, the BBC was starved, the Greater London Council abolished, gas and water privatised, the film industry deprived of subsidy and tax incentive and so in effect abolished, Shaftesbury Avenue was largely torn down, and great architectural sites reduced to rubble and replaced with big glass tower blocks and yuppy apartments, Fleet Street was mortally wounded along with its printing unions, its presses computerised and the *Times* surrendered to Rupert Murdoch, Liverpool was ruined as a dockside city, British Leyland sold to Germany, Jaguar sold to General Motors, country rail lines privatised, the great choir-singing culture of the Welsh coal valleys battered to its knees, Scottish ship-building abolished and Northern Ireland so provoked that London became an IRA war zone, public housing was sold off and the income from North Sea oil largely spent on the amount required to feed the consequent unemployed.

'There is no alternative,' cried the lady who was not for turning. 'The politics of TINA (There Is No Alternative)' was the name it was given.

All this was for a long time presented as a triumph. On paper, the trade balance, the credit rating, the currency of Britain were improved, and union power smashed. In fact, all of Britain's essential services were worse, prices crippling, wages lower, and unemployment enormous; divorce, drug addiction and suicide went up and burglary became rife; the property boom and bust was a social catastrophe, with people stuck with mortgages they could never pay off; and all of Britain north of Birmingham was an economic wreck, the proud industrial towns of Yorkshire and Scotland decaying ruins, the fine films *Brassed Off* and *The Full Monty* a fairly accurate portrait of what had come to pass.

And after four elections – one of them won by the war in the Falklands, three of them because of Labour's divisions, the voting system and the constant unfair assault on Foot and Kinnock by the British media – the Tory government was swept from power in 1996 by a Labour majority of 179, and the Tory Party fell into crisis and may not rise again. The bitterness of a riven Britain will keep it out of power for at least twenty years, the experts assess, and maybe longer.

So economic rationalism in Britain has been, for the moment at least, a political disaster. In that country at least it seems it cannot succeed as long as people have, and exercise, the vote.

47

Hold onto that thought.

Economic rationalism as a system and democracy as a system are incompatible, eventually incompatible. And one of them has to go.

48

Economic anorexia failed likewise in Canada, where the slashing, burning and privatising governments of Mulroney and Campbell were, after they introduced a GST (the equivalent of VAT), reduced in parliamentary membership from 163 to two.

49

In New Zealand, similarly, where economic rationalism was introduced at dizzying speed by the new Labour Treasurer Roger Douglas (and thus was nicknamed Rogernomics) the Labour government survived three terms while its representation fell from fifty-six seats to twenty-nine seats, after the popular Prime Minister David Lange, appalled at what was happening to his nation, resigned in disgust.

The right-wing National Party replaced Labour in government in 1993 and pressed on with Rogernomics with Thatcherite zeal. As a result of this, the governing party split, and the Labour Party split, and in the elections of 1996 a populist party, New Zealand First, and the Nationals joined in an abrasive coalition. At the time of writing, this coalition had fractured into two more party groupings – its vote was down to thirty-two percent, and it looked certain to lose the imminent election of 1999.

50

In Australia, similarly, where rationalism was pursued with rather more merciful provisos and mitigations by the Hawke and Keating governments, the ruling Labor Party's vote fell from forty-eight percent to thirty-nine percent, and in the traumatic landslide of 1996 it lost more seats – thirty-two out of eighty-one – than it had in all of its federal history.

The incoming right-wing Howard government, more Thatcherite than Thatcher, pursued economic rationalism with punishing zeal, and in two years its vote fell from forty-seven percent to thirty-four percent, then thirty-eight percent, and a new party, One Nation, based on a primitive drumbeat of populational fundamentalism (better known as White Australia) rose to engulf it and sorely damage Australia's trade in the increasingly irritable neighbouring region of South-East Asia. At the time of writing it seemed likely the Howard government would fall, and either a chastened protectionist Labor Party or a rabid, semi-fascist One Nation Party replace it.

51

Throughout Europe, the rise of similar racist and protectionist parties has dogged the onrushing zealotry of economic rationalist governments, and threatens on every polling day to bring them down.

Economic rationalism and democracy don't mix.

Follow the thread.

52

The most dramatic example of all this is modern Russia. And because of its recent communist history, the most telling.

By 1988, when the author first went there, the Soviet Union's Russia, under Gorbachev and perestroika, was an interesting mixed bag. As rumoured, there were frequent unpredictable shortages – of toilet paper, soap, contraceptives. Contraception was rare and abortion frequent. Many women had had six or seven abortions. Housing was a nightmare of confined spaces in big apartment blocks, with dining rooms doubling as bedrooms for the principal couple, and a widowed mother-in-law, babushka, occupying the one room at the back. Divorce was rife, and open marriages, and a surprising amount of part-time prostitution among otherwise loyal and caring wives. The black market was everywhere, and a brisk, almost universal trade in forged currency. There was a passion for American dollars, which could only be spent in shops that Russians could not enter unless accompanied by a foreigner. Wages were weighted according to hardship: thus an old female street sweeper made more than a nuclear physicist, a fireman more than a professor of literature.

But . . . the Moscow, Kiev, St Petersburg, Odessa and Yalta of those years boasted (and I have witnessed it) the best live theatre in the world, to which you could go for the equivalent of forty cents. They had as well the best urban transport systems, the best parks, the best ballet companies – both classical and modern – very good opera, and by far the best circuses on the planet. Almost everyone in Russia was highly educated, and articulate in Tolstoy and Shakespeare and Einstein and Orson Welles to a level unimaginable in America, and attainable elsewhere only in Switzerland or Scotland in the nineteen fifties.

The cinema was astonishing. The great studios of Kiev turned out five hundred feature films a year – in one city alone – and hundred-piece orchestras on full pay sat round the studio playing cards. One actor had played Stalin seventeen times in three years.

Intellectual life was rich in the boulevard cafes, and freedom of speech unfettered. Former government ministers were grilled every night on television by fearless interviewers.

Because of the worthless currency, no-one could travel much outside the Communist bloc, although holidays to India and the Black Sea were possible. Many ordinary Russians had a dacha, a rundown wooden summer house in a rural setting, and most had a vegetable patch outside the city.

Everyone had a job, and everyone had a roof.

No-one slept on the streets.

The streets were safe, the safest in Europe. There was almost no crime, except the occasional drunken brawl over a woman or a cultural judgment. Some people froze to death in winter parks, but not for want of accommodation, only excess of drunkenness.

Health care was free. Electricity cost a dollar a month. Fruit and vegetables were amazingly cheap. Luxury goods like CDs amazingly dear.

It was a civilisation, in short, comparable with others. It had its frustrations but also its glories – like the Kiev orchestra playing Mozart and, for balance, Salieri to an unpaying audience in an autumn park at twilight.

The Soviet Union's Russia was okay. The average living standard was that, I suppose, of a kindergarten teacher in Murwillumbah, or Peoria, or Clacton-on-Sea, with five free tickets a week to world class concerts, plays, recitals and circuses. You could be happy in Soviet Russia under Gorbachev, and many were.

Then Yeltsin got in, and economic rationalism, and everything improved. Improved out of sight.

53

People are now evicted from the flats they once had as a right. They are begging on the streets and sleeping in the pedestrian tunnels – parents, children, mothers-in-law. The streets are a growing nightmare of armed gangsters, and even the richest tourists are unsafe. The Bolshoi Ballet is closing, the film industry in recession, the orchestra's members busking. Inflation is at one thousand percent and, as in Germany in the twenties, the life savings of the old will barely buy a week's groceries. Thousands of mine workers have not been paid their wages for three years. Local regions like Chechnya and Georgia have attempted armed uprisings and been bombed and starved back into submission.

Sacked air force colonels, applying the pleasing new rules of the free market and the level playing field, are selling nuclear weapons under the counter to Pakistani generals and Arab terrorists. Fascist parties are on the upswing. The Communist Party is making a comeback. Boris Yeltsin is begging the International Monetary Fund for even more billions to deal with the consequences of his economic brilliance – his economic correctness. The artistic abundance that was long the glory of Russia is now a price-slashed ruin that must pay its way (and, to be fair, some companies can, like the ceaselessly world-touring Moscow Circus) or go under. Many magnificent choirs and orchestras and local opera companies are in liquidation.

And the duly elected members of the Russian parliament, the Duma, who protested against these measures were unconstitutionally treated as Red Revolutionaries and dealt with very severely. Their parliament was bombarded and set on fire, and forty-nine of them shot dead as they stumbled out of the flames. The world press called these democratically elected fellows the Hardliners, and the men shooting them on Czar Boris's orders the Reformists. When Gorbachev tried to run for office again, in the Presidential election of 1995, his face and speeches were banned from television on Yeltsin's orders.

Yeltsin has now sacked his entire cabinet, and drinks heavily, and howls for more and more money from overseas agencies. Economic rationalism, in short, has come to Russia. And now all is chaos, and warring mafias, and recrimination, and people freezing in the streets.

At the time of writing, Yeltsin had sacked his entire *second* cabinet and was himself awaiting impeachment, forced retirement or army coup.

54

All this is known.

Yet no commentators – or almost no commentators – have said or written the bleeding obvious: that the average Russian or Ukrainian or Chechnyan lived better and more securely under the command economy of Gorbachev's communism than the 'freed-up' economy of Yeltsin's capitalism, capitalism with its hungry jackal face. That sleeping in a centrally heated flat, however small, is better than sleeping in a pedestrian tunnel. That having a job, however dull, is better than begging or busking or mugging for your bread. That an inflation rate of nothing or one percent is better than an inflation rate of one thousand percent. That working for wages is better than working for no wages. And so on.

For to admit that might raise the question of whether or not communism sometimes has virtues and capitalism sometimes has faults, and that would never do.

All that most commentators will admit is that Russia is going through a rough patch right now, but is on the right track, and in the long run all will be well.

In the long run, said Lord Keynes, we are all dead.

And in even the short run there are thousands now

dead because of Yeltsin's drunken rationalist craziness who would have lived under Gorbachev sobriety.

Economic rationalism kills.

55

But these confronting failures in practice mean little to the university-subsidised, corporation-pampered and computer-pallid gladiators of the new order. All that is proved by these luckless examples, they assert, is that the theory is not being pursued hard enough.

A Britain socially and spiritually devastated by Thatcher has therefore not been Thatcherising hard enough.

A Scotland that in 1996 elected not one Tory to the House of Commons and voted hugely for devolution in the August referendum is plainly ungrateful for the policy benefits that are just around the corner.

The facts matter little to the Grand Theoreticians. The zealotry goes on.

Harder, go in harder.

56

And different standards are applied.

Lyndon Johnson's Great Society, for instance, which poured money into the black ghettos of America, and hoped to uplift the underclass into self-respect and educational enthusiasm and some promise of career and community was pronounced a failure and a waste and a scandal by these Grand Theoreticians after only five years; and, under Nixon, its demolition begun.

Thatcherism, by contrast, after eighteen years, still needs and still deserves more time to prove itself.

Thatcherism, they say, wasn't applied hard enough. This time no more Mr Nice Guy.

57

There used to be an expression that was applied to this kind of thinking.

It was called flogging a dead horse.

Expendable as Kleenex

58

Let us now ask a pertinent question. What is economic rationalism up to? What is it driving at? What is its vision for the future? What does it imagine it is creating?

The prophesied scenario seems to be the following.

That by the year 2025 (say) all the nations of the world will be free of tariff barriers and competing equally on a level playing field and all *winning*.

Let me run that past you again.

All one hundred and ninety-three nations of the world will be fighting each other for markets and all of them winning the fight.

59

They will be doing this, the computer-pallid gladiators assert, by specialising. Some nations will specialise in CD-ROMs, some in canned fruit, some in solar-powered motor scooters, some in cheap footwear, some in spare parts for space rockets, some, possibly, in heroin – or under-the-counter nuclear weapons. There will be profit for all, and jobs for all – or nearly all – once the market is free and lovely and global. Unfettered, energetic and rational.

60

Now, a moron can see (but not an economic rationalist, discuss) that a race with one hundred and ninety-three starters might have some losers.

That some countries might start out in CD-ROMS but be outclassed or out-invented by the eager boffins of northern California or Kyoto. Or try to outdo the Volvo on the world market, and ingloriously fail.

What does such a country do then? What do its political leaders do to cover their shame – apart from sack a few advisers? What do they do, and say they will do, when running for re-election?

Some of them will put their tariffs back up, surely, to protect their buffeted local industries and products.

Won't they? Surely they will.

And what will happen then?

61

Well, a rival country, outraged at this breach of treaty, will respond – won't it? – by putting *its* tariffs back up on certain embattled goods. And a third country, outraged, will do the same.

And before you know it, there will be tariff barriers back up all over the world. And, in each country, local industries reviving. Bottling companies. Brickworks. Local refrigerators and radios. Local automobiles. Local cheese and wines and biscuits and beers and mineral water.

Some of the goods will be shoddy. Some of the wages will be low. Many of the businesses will be small and the markets local. The way they used to be.

And many more people will be in work. And many more people buying things.

Many more customers, back from abolishment.

Many more people trading.

Economies exist because people trade, and not the other way round.

62

And all the necessary hardship of the previous fifty years will have been for nothing. All the Thatcherite and Yeltsinite brutality. All the Blairite 'compassion, but with a hard edge'. And the Keatingite 'Big Picture'.

Nothing.

Worse than nothing, in fact.

For there will be hundreds of millions of lives ruined, and hopes dashed, and towns emptied, and barren farms windblown, in pursuit of a baseless fantasy.

If a baseless fantasy is all it is.

Because it could be something worse.

We'll talk about that later.

63

Try this thought for a minute.

One of the more hectically reiterated subclauses of the salespitch of economic rationalism is that globalisation – that is, company expansion overseas – brings jobs.

In Australia, lately, when the grassroots revolt One Nation voted rabidly against the destruction by free marketeers of rural communities, the defenders of rationalism, the Prime Minister and others, once again said globalisation brings jobs and cited as their prime example McDonald's.

How many young people, they asked, young people now at work in McDonald's, would be otherwise unemployed? How many young people who thus get a start in life, thanks to globalisation?

It sounds persuasive, till you realise what they are

saying is that if there were no McDonald's, no Australian would eat hamburgers.

Yet this is not so. Before McDonald's came the hamburger was a favourite Australian fast food. Prime Minister Chifley referred to it in his famous oration, The Light on the Hill, in 1949.

There were three or four hamburger joints in most country towns. Young people worked in them and other young people hung out in them. They often had jukeboxes and pinball machines. Girls were picked up in them, and taken away in cars. Some of them were attached to drive-in cinemas.

Families did not come to them in great numbers, it is true, but that was because in those days families could afford better food. They could afford better food because there were more jobs. There were more jobs because Australian industries and local communities were protected by tariffs from concerns like McDonald's that sold Australians cheap, third-rate goods and sent the profits overseas.

And if there were fewer jobs as an aggregate in the hamburger business, there were other things that young people could do. They could work in the local bottling factory where, before the massive market agglomeration of Coca Cola, there were local cordials – Lismore Cordials, Ipswich Soft Drinks, Halls,

Mynor – many of them involved with local pride. There were local factories that made radios and furniture and shoes and bicycles. There were things for young people to do.

There are fewer jobs for young people now, thanks to globalisation.

The McDonald's argument is a lie.

64

For the globalisation process works, as a generality, like this.

In the great city of Kiev (for argument's sake), capital of Ukraine, which is now no longer a part of the Soviet Union, but an utterly separate entity from Russia, there are hundreds of thousands of young men newly jobless and angry and drunk. The social and economic structures that, under communism, sustained and employed and accommodated them have been abolished or privatised, and the massive resulting inflation has robbed them of whatever savings they or their family once had.

These young men are prepared to work for twenty dollars a week.

And the executives of Coca Cola do their sums. They decide that if all the Coca Cola bottling in Europe (for argument's sake) is done in Kiev, they will be able to serve the entire European market (with underpaid Russian truck drivers delivering all over) more cheaply than they do now.

So they sack the young men working in France, Germany, Spain and so on for decent wages.

Coca Cola has become more efficient and competitive.

They can sell Coca Cola more cheaply now, more cheaply than Pepsi Cola. And they have more money to advertise it.

The young men thus retrenched in France, Germany, Spain and so on go on the dole, or into street crime, or busking.

The young men now employed in Ukraine have hardly any money to live on. Coca Cola, for instance, is a luxury item for them. And meanwhile the local economies and the local communities in France, Germany and Spain are damaged.

But the price of Coca Cola shares, of course, goes up. And the board of directors is rightly pleased.

Then Indonesia goes bust, and the company executives tell the board of directors that there are young men and women in Jakarta willing to work for ten dollars a week.

This, they all agree, is a great improvement on twenty dollars a week.

And the bottling factories in Australia, New Zealand, Japan and the Philippines are closed, and the young men, retrenched, go into crime and busking and drugs and despair. Or they leave home and wander vainly in search of a job.

And the price of Coca Cola shares goes up. And the top executives all get a bonus. And the board of directors is delighted. They award themselves a bonus too.

Because it's working out fine for *them,* if very badly for those labourers no longer on their assembly line because they are no longer essential to their operations, whose bottom line is always profit, greater profit.

And the rich get richer (oh yes). And the poor despair.

65

If you were an astronaut looking down on the planet Earth and, from a divine perspective, overviewing this process, you would probably crunch the figures on your computer and summarise it thus.

That the greed of a few hundred thousand shareholders now outweighs – and will always outweigh, and should outweigh, because of the way the world is ordered now – the need and suffering of *five billion* ordinary people, with rent to pay, and children to clothe and send to school. This is the way the system works. And this is the way it ought to work. This is economically rational.

And some people, according to the system, are precious, and so are their priorities; and other people are not so precious, whatever their priorities.

Some people are as disposable as Kleenex.

66

There used to be another name for this international process. Its economic methods were slightly different, and its geographical strategy was slightly different. But its bottom line was the same.

Its name was slavery.

67

Slavery was a major ingredient of the world economy for most of recorded history. It was widespread (and famously present in the USA) one hundred and thirty years ago, and it still persists in some parts of Africa and the Arabian peninsula and the Indian sub-continent.

Its usual method was a raiding party on a coastal village, and the kidnapping of able-bodied young men and handsome young women and their transport in chains to another country. Some would die on the voyage – of grief, confinement, disease, gang rape or murder. Those who survived would be auctioned and, if a male, put to work in a mine or on a plantation, or, if a female, put in domestic service, with duties that included sexually satisfying the master and other family members.

The slaves were given shacks to live in. They were permitted to cohabit, sometimes to marry. A husband and wife, however, could be separated, and separated for life, if sold again to different owners. Their children could be sold off too, and they would never see them again.

They had enough to eat. They were not allowed to leave the plantation. If they misbehaved they might be castrated, or have one hand cut off, or be flogged with a lash a hundred times. They were allowed to practise religion, sing songs, and tell stories from memory of their homeland and clan. Those who were lucky were allowed to learn to read.

In modern times the methods are a little different. The slaves stay home. The raiding parties are corporation executives who buy up land and local infrastructure and offer 'competitive' wages to those lucky enough to secure employment. For competitive wages read slave wages. It's an easy enough concept to grasp.

They have enough to eat. They can practise religion and sing songs. Their women often sexually service their masters as before, that's if they know what's good for them. They can travel out of the district in theory but they usually can't afford to.

And their lives can be wrecked at any moment by a sacking or a factory closure. A husband can be forced to separate from his wife, if his wife still has a job, by seeking work a thousand miles away.

If they plead for better wages or safer conditions they can be sacked. There are plenty more wage-slaves where they come from. If they go on strike they can be imprisoned, or in Australia fined in the millions for imperilling their bosses' level of profit.

And their lives, like those of slaves, can be capriciously distorted overnight, their families sundered, their houses taken, their children banished, their hurt unimaginable.

Many get drunk, and then hang themselves in gaol. Many more despair, and divorce, and lead withered souring lives. The company shareholders, however, do very well indeed. If they do not they sell up that factory and move on, and do well elsewhere with a new set of wage-slaves on even lower wages, leaving the last lot in penury and rage and grief.

68

One man's profit is another man's loss, discuss.

A global economy's profit is many, many people's loss.

And not just the customer's.

69

In modern times there have been many examples of adapted forms of slavery. Five perhaps will suffice.

70

In Guatemala in 1946 Ubico, dictator of that country and a close ally of the American multinational company United Fruit, was replaced in a free election by Arevalo, a philosophy professor and social democrat. Encouraged by this democratic upsurge the Guatemalan employees of United Fruit (whose annual budget was larger than that of Guatemala) went on strike for more money.

'Selfishly,' reports Gore Vidal, a witness, 'they had wanted to be paid $1.50 a day for their interesting work.'

This alerted United Fruit, the CIA and the American government to the evil spectre of communism in Central America. If they wanted as much as a dollar fifty a day (eighteen dollars a day in current money), then Stalin must be in back of it somewhere, organising things.

The workers got their $1.50 a day, but trouble was brewing.

In 1953 came further proof of the Stalin thesis. Arevalo's freely elected successor Arbenz expropriated some of United Fruit's unused land, and gave it to one hundred thousand Guatemalan families.

'Arbenz,' reports Vidal, 'paid the company what he thought was a fair, if humorous price: their own evaluation of the land for tax purposes.'

The CIA went into action, got together an army, and bombed Guatemala City. Arbenz resigned and the American ambassador, Puerifroy, hand-picked a successor from the ranks of the army, and gave him a list of 'communists' to be shot. He complied. Guatemala has been a bloodbath ever since. The United Fruit company is still its ruler. Its employees now, on average, get thirteen dollars a day.

If this is not slavery, enforced by a foreign power, it is something pretty close to it.

71

In the Philippines until the fall of Marcos it was a routine act of domestic economics for a peasant family to sell an eleven-year-old daughter into a Manila whorehouse –

sometimes for forty dollars, sometimes a hundred – and for her to contract AIDS there and die of it by the age of twenty or twenty-five, after passing it on to customers.

If this is not slavery, it is something pretty close to it. And a perfect example of market economics.

It was not uncommon either for the prostituted daughter to send money from her earnings back to her impoverished family. The family would accept it, but never invite her to visit, lest she bring shame on their house.

72

In a not dissimilar transaction, lonely and sexually frustrated Australian men could write away to a marriage broker and, after perusing a photograph, acquire a Filipino wife by merely paying her fare to Australia. She would marry him and live in his caravan or shack and slave for him and endure his beatings unaware of her rights under Australian law.

If this is not slavery – the purchase of a person for unlimited use without recompense – it is something very close to it.

73

For most of the twentieth century it has been routine for undereducated Mexicans or Guatemalans or

Panamanians to cross the Rio Grande by night and thus enter America illegally and live there, fearful of exposure and forced repatriation, working as farm hands or domestic servants for a third or a quarter of the wages of legal Americans and sometimes no wages whatever, only their food and lodging. The threat of denunciation to the authorities by their 'owners' keeps them docile, hard-working and, if so desired, sexually available to the master of the house.

Some of them run away back to Mexico, or Guatemala or Panama. Most do not.

If this is not slavery – the forcible possession and exploitation of a choiceless human being who stays your abject vassal under threat of unthinkable punishment – it is something pretty close to it.

74

In Australia from the eighteen nineties to the nineteen seventies babies and children of indigenous parentage, those who had lighter skins, were forcibly taken away from their weeping mothers by government officials and raised in church institutions or fostered out to suitable white couples, often on farm properties. Their mothers' letters were not passed on. The children's letters begging their mothers to come and get them were likewise never posted, and no phone calls were allowed. Many were told they could go home for holidays, and none were allowed to. Many did not see their mother again for forty years; many never saw her again.

In the institutions their treatment varied. But many were forced to work long hours, scrubbing and sweeping before and after their ill-taught school lessons, and many, both male and female, routinely raped at night or otherwise assaulted, by priests and male nurses. Most were beaten. Most were made to pray. Few were comforted when upset. Few were hugged or caressed, except in the course of sexual capture and servitude.

Many of the girls were put to work in homesteads as domestic help. They were fed, not paid, or paid very little, and often impregnated by the grazier. One girl was impregnated five times and had five babies. All five babies were taken away from her and put in institutions, institutions like the one she was raised in. She became very depressed, and was in due course fired for her attitude, and another girl, in her early teens, adopted in her place.

This is a major scandal in Australian history, and has its parallels in the British children brought without their parents' permission to Australia and raised and brutalised in similar institutions.

In each process, as in slavery, there was the forced removal from a home environment and lifelong exile from it. In each, as in slavery, there was a lack of choice in the work they would do in life. In each, as in slavery, there was hard unpaid work in childhood commingled sometimes, not always, with rape.

The youngest of the children so treated are now in their late twenties. This is a very recent story. Some of the older ones are dead of suicide.

What staggered Sir Ronald Wilson, the chief investigator of these recent atrocities, was how widespread they were.

If this is not – or was not – child slavery, it was something pretty close to it.

75

In the chain gangs of the United States in the early part of the century, in the privatised prisons of Victoria today, in the work-for-the-dole schemes of Australia (where some teenagers on the dole are forced, though others are not, to work for their subsistence entitlements), slavery, or something like it, is routinely practised with government approval, the governments of western countries. In every migrant enclave there is an illegally imported relative exploited and overworked.

Slavery continues.

Slavery is economically rational; and it always was.

76

From the above examples it is pretty clear that the tendency of human beings to exploit, harass and ill-treat their fellow creatures is a common one, and few appeals to Christian values or humanitarian decency will be greatly heeded when there is money to be made out of ill-treated workers, and less money to be made out of well-treated ones.

The history of child labour in the deeply religious nineteenth century illustrates this, with children four years old in the cotton mills working fourteen hours a day and dropping dead from exhaustion before they reached their teens. And children of a similar age being hanged by the neck until dead for stealing money for food when their families asked them to.

If there is a merciful tendency in human beings – and there may well sometimes be – it is not universal, and in some societies not common. And people involved in the making of money, money in great amounts, do not often have it.

The myth we are asked to believe in is that economic rationalists do.

77

A vivid illustration of this has only lately come to light in the great banks of Switzerland.

After the details of the Holocaust became known – the confiscation of wealth and property, slave labour, slaughter in gas chambers, the theft from corpses of gold teeth, the boiling down of bodies for soap – it also became known that much of the confiscated property lay, in money and gold bullion, in the vaults of Swiss banks, where it was put by Jews now dead or by Nazi officials against the day of defeat.

Instead of looking for its rightful owners or their relatives and giving it back, the Swiss banks kept it and invested it. They looked on it as a windfall from a great hurricane of history. Their windfall.

And Jews who had lost their families and might have had, at least, some family money in recompense were denied it. It was stolen from them by those most respectable of institutions, the Swiss banks of Geneva and Zurich and Berne.

If these proper institutions can rob and pillage the Second World War's least fortunate group of people, who can we say for certain will not do likewise? American businessmen? English businessmen? Australian businessmen? Hungarian businessmen?

Give me a break.

78

For it is such people who, without exception, enacted and perfected that modern variant on slavery, mechanisation.

About a hundred years ago it became plain that an efficient machine was a preferable employee to a fallible worker.

The machine did not ask for annual holidays. Or sick leave. Or better pay and conditions. It did not have smokos or lunch breaks or loud office Christmas parties. And it worked uncomplainingly twenty-four hours a day.

Once this became known the sacking of workers and their replacement by machines began.

Farm workers were replaced by combine harvesters. Horse-and-coach drivers by T-model Fords. Individual seamstresses by machines that sewed faster. Great numbers of entertainers in town halls and pubs by fewer entertainers heard over the wireless, or seen on cinema screens. Switchboard operators by automatic telephones. Receptionists by automatic telephones. Railway cafe waitresses by food-dispensing machines. Ticket sellers by ticket-selling machines. Bank tellers by autobanks.

All these improvements were economically rational, in that they increased the profits of companies.

All took jobs from ordinary people. Jobs that will never come back.

And yet we are told that economic rationalist practice, within the free market, is good for jobs. More jobs will come, we are told, when we get through this difficult but necessary phase. Just a few more years of pain, and all will be well. Gain for everyone. Soon the aeroplanes loaded with refrigerators and mixmasters will fly in out of the rainbow and there will be goodies for everyone.

Who believes this anymore?

Yet John Howard, the Australian Prime Minister, says privatised companies would never act in a way that is unfair to Australian citizens.

And John Howard is an honourable man.

79

A fair measure of how global corporations act, and how brazen they are in their actions, may be found in the archives of Coca Cola.

After Coca Cola, the drink, was banned because of its addictive ingredient cocaine, a second formula, based on caffeine, was sought by its executives.

One man, an employee of the Schaefer Alkaloid Company of New Jersey, devised and perfected the still secret formula that became, and remains, a world bestseller.

Guess how much this man, whose name is not easy to discover, was given as a reward for his efforts, this man who saved and enriched the company beyond the dreams of Midas?

Nothing.

No shares, no bonus.

He was a company employee, it was argued, and he was only doing his job.

80

Another example is Ub Iwerks.

Initially the genius behind Walt Disney, Iwerks invented all the methods of animation, and many of the characters, that made Walt's company first in its field. He fell out with Disney, almost certainly over money (Walt was notoriously stingy), resigned, and came back years later asking for a big creative role in the company.

He was given a job as an assembly-line colouring-in man, and in due course resigned again, and died broke.

Disney owed him everything. A share of the take for his brilliant mentor would have cost him personally nothing. But he made no such offer, and the originating auteur of the Disney billions died broke.

81

Louis Augustin Le Prince, likewise, was badly treated by Thomas Alva Edison.

An Englishman from Birmingham, Le Prince invented the first movie camera in 1888, and took it to Edison to offer him a part in its development. No contract was signed, but Le Prince left behind a camera to show Edison, in good faith, how it worked.

Edison had him murdered (or so it is powerfully argued), pushed off a train in southern France. He stole the design, and fought Le Prince's angry family in court for eleven years against their just claims for remuneration.

In 1902 the court proclaimed that Edison was not, in fact, the inventor of cinema and that others, Le Prince among them, had a more convincing claim on the invention.

But by then the Edison studios were the prime source of cameras and projectors.

The Edison Company was awarded by history the equivalent of millions.

Louis Le Prince, the creator of world cinema, was awarded a broken neck, and oblivion.

Cut to black. The end.

This is the way big corporations treat their underlings,

and their small competitors. Or this is the way that some of them do.

82

Yet the ever-optimistic John Howard (Prime Minister, as I write this, of Australia) says that Telstra, which has already sacked twenty-five thousand of its employees, will if totally privatised not – and not ever, never ever – disadvantage its customers, even if by disadvantaging them it makes more money for its shareholders.

Not now. Not in the year 2100. Not *ever*.

And John Howard is an honourable man.

And all the linesmen and repairmen of Telstra will get other jobs, somewhere else in the workforce, in other companies already retrenching workers.

You have his word on that.

Somewhere, out there, is work for everybody who wants it.

You better believe it.

Get on your bike.

83

A more chilling variant (perhaps) on the above is company expansion – the imperial tendency in big corporations, or globalisation as it is known.

Take the ever-interesting example of Rupert Murdoch.

Murdoch, born Australian, discovered early that if you have an Australian newspaper – called, for argument's sake, the *Australian* – you need to have on staff a London correspondent to keep up with what is happening, in detail, in England. You likewise have to have a New York correspondent, a Middle East correspondent, a Hong Kong correspondent, a South Pacific correspondent, and so on.

If, however, you own a London newspaper as well as an Australian newspaper, you no longer need a London correspondent for the Australian paper, nor an Australian correspondent for the London paper; you have one already on the local staff, and all you have to do is reprint his copy. So each new newspaper you buy, the fewer overall staff you need.

Most global corporations work on this principle. The bigger the company, the fewer jobs there are in that whole field of endeavour. And the less competition.

This makes a lot of sense to Murdoch, and the figures, for him, add up. He has proved this by acquiring most of the newspapers and broadcast satellites of the world, plus Twentieth Century Fox.

But . . . the catch with Murdochism is that editor

after editor, and television executive after television executive, has to conform to the sometimes wayward ideas of that one driven man – and, though not always, to abandon much of his conscience to do so.

He must, for instance, praise Margaret Thatcher undeviatingly, and attack Prince Charles and Teddy Kennedy. He must persuade a stupendous number of impressionable young women to bare their ample bosoms on page three. He must at all times deride and attack the Labour Party leader Neil Kinnock, calling him a 'Welsh Windbag' and a mere glove puppet of his wife Glenys. He must abandon Fleet Street, sack all his technical staff, and move through howling picket lines to the Isle of Dogs.

He must, moreover, during the House of Commons election of 1987 run a piece entitled 'Why I am Voting for Neil Kinnock, by Joseph Stalin', claiming it is a transcript from a spirit medium in touch with that long renowned dead villain, and another piece entitled, 'Why I am Voting for Margaret Thatcher, by Winston Churchill.'

He must then, when times change, find reasons for backing Labour and its impressive (and very right-wing) new leader Tony Blair, and bucket the excesses of Thatcherism that are now so unpopular.

This leads not only to bad journalism, and the sacking or retirement of some good and honourable writers, and the alcoholism of others, but also to a culture of low standards, of peephole exposés and Princess Di sex gossip, of bribing convicted criminals and their wives and friends to tell all for six-figure sums and the tainting worldwide (eventually world-wide) of the name of journalism itself.

'Thatcherism,' Lord Puttnam said to the author in 1989, 'may have only ten years to live. But Murdochism has a thousand years.'

Rupert Murdoch, the man, may not be all bad (he funded, after all, the fine film *Titanic)*, but his world-bestriding ambition and imperial control of what the world may know and, to some extent, may think, is not the best of outcomes for humankind. In his born-again-Christian, newly divorced and feverishly puritan old age he may lead the world in strange directions while still pursuing with fire and sword his boyhood goals of the crushing of both world socialism and the British Royal Family, crushing all competition in his chosen field and making or breaking governments according to his whim.

He is the most powerful man in history, probably, and needs watching.

He is, of course, a profound and fervent supporter

of economic rationalism, and yet is bent on slaughtering all competition in his field, and every field he enters. Are all global companies, one wonders, bent on the same end?

Are they therefore friends of competition, or its most voracious enemies?

Keep that question in mind.

84

'The foremost problem now facing a modern economy,' said Syd Hickman, political adviser to Kim Beazley and author, 'is what do you do with dumb blokes?'

Dumb blokes, he said, used to hold the horses and on bicycles deliver the telegrams, and with scythes cut down the sugar cane, and with axes cut down the forests, and with sharp knives cut the throats of bellowing cows in the slaughterhouse, and work in the bottle factory or the brickworks. Dumb blokes would drink a bit, shoot rabbits, play pool, fish, get married, have children, argue, grow old.

They had a life. And they don't have it any more.

It's different for dumb girls. They still have the work – or much of the work – they used to have. As receptionists, waitresses, salesgirls in big stores, nannies, masseuses, prostitutes, chars.

But for dumb blokes there is no easy way out. What is to happen to them?

85

Well, it depends what kind of society you are in. In a police state there is a greater need for police. And dumb blokes get a lot of work in the new expanded police force, protecting politicians from assassination, and arresting dissidents, and breaking up riots and torturing political prisoners. In a society keen on bull-fighting, there is a fair bit of work to do round bulls, and horses, and crowd control, and selling ice-creams, and running up and repairing gold costumes, and washing the bloodstains off. In a society keen on football there are football scholarships to the universities and football clubs in every significant suburb where dumb blokes with big shoulders might find work and fulfilment, and retirement jobs as doormen.

In a warrior society like Sparta or Israel there is always a place in the army. In a society keen on boxing there is work in gymnasiums in most big towns. In a society that has banned boxing, however, there is no work in this field at all. In a warrior society forbidden to ever go to war again, like Japan, the young men have to seek fulfilment elsewhere, by eating a lot, perhaps, and becoming sumo wrestlers, or working a lot, and becoming company executives.

86

So it depends what kind of society you have, and choose to have – and there *is* a choice – and what kind of priorities that society has, and believes in.

If the society, like the Gorbachev Soviet Union, believes in jobs for everyone, jobs for everyone as a first priority, there may well *be* jobs for everyone. If the society, like Yeltsin's Russia, believes in profits for the nouveau mafia, profits for the nouveau mafia as a first priority, there will not be jobs for everyone. And there will be inflation of one thousand percent, and street begging, and families freezing in pedestrian tunnels, and orchestras going out of business, and so on.

And dumb blokes drinking too much and freezing to death in parks in winter.

This is not a necessary outcome, however, and it need not even be a likely one.

Pay attention.

87

In the European Union the component nations are signatories of what is called the Social Charter.

This is a list of the standards below which the nations will not go.

These include:

- All workers have the right to equal opportunities and equal treatment in matters of employment and occupation without discrimination on the grounds of sex.
- Workers have the right to take part in the determination and improvement of their working conditions and working environment.
- The right as well to access to employment, protection against dismissal and occupational resettlement.
- The right to be informed regularly or at the appropriate time and in a comprehensible way about the economic and financial situation of the company employing them.
- The right to be consulted in good time on proposed decisions which could substantially affect their interests or their continued employment.
- The right to the determination and the improvement of their working conditions, work organisation and working environment.
- The right to the protection of their health and safety.
- The right to the organisation of social and socio-cultural services and facilities.

- The right to the supervision of the regulations on these matters.
- Every elderly person has the right to social protection.

These enforced provisos apply regardless, curiously, of the profit levels of the multinational companies at work in Europe.

If the profit levels of these companies go down because of the Social Charter, tough.

If because of the profit levels the companies decide to ignore the Social Charter, they are thrown out of Europe.

It happens.

For the EU still believes in a concept of minimal civilisation that is not underminable by concepts of ever-rising profit, or capriciously alterable by the greed of shareholders.

Civilisation above all.

88

Now the EU idea of civilisation is all very fine – and better certainly than the Australian one, which has lately refused to agree to the clauses quoted above – but there are bigger questions that it has not answered.

One of these is why any company's profits should be, theoretically, limitless.

Why they cannot, like wages, be pegged.

89

For wages are never limitless, except perhaps in the Hollywood star system. Charges are never limitless, even in downtown carparks. Taxes are certainly never limitless. Rates have limits that are local and political. The speed of cars is limited on most highways and all suburban streets, even though most cars are built to go much faster than that. The amount of alcohol you can drink is limited when you are at the wheel of a car. The types of guns you can own are limited now in several countries, to bring down the number of murders in hours of drunkenness or ill-temper. The punishment that judges can mete out to criminals, the length and severity of sentences, is limited, in the interests of civilisation.

In each case there is an agreed-on, negotiated upper limit of what is reasonable to charge or pay for the goods or services provided.

Under economic rationalism, however, profits can be as big as the earth and sky. Whatever the consequences, the level of profit has no bounds.

90

And the board of directors, moreover, is not doing its work if it does not double the company's profits every four or five years.

In order to do so, it sacks and sacks and sacks its component people, and damages or ruins their lives and grievously overworks the people remaining, and harries and corrodes their lives as well.

And for what? What is being gained here, at the cost of so much human suffering?

It's not a change in lifestyle for the board of directors. They still have their Porsches and skiing holidays.

It's not an improvement in the company product. It, *almost by definition,* is getting worse.

No, it's an ego surge in those board members now staring at all those extra noughts on the page. A certain chest-beating contentment that they have prevailed, though so many others have lost, in a battle for dominance. A certain sadistic satisfaction, perhaps.

Is this worth destroying society for?

91

A just democratic system would confiscate all company profits over twenty-two percent.

Or nineteen percent. Or twenty-five percent after inflation. Whatever.

It would have to be instituted worldwide and it would be hard to police, but it would possibly stop the economic slaughter that is everywhere.

Hold onto that thought. And follow the thread.

92

One of the worst consequences of the greedy profiteering of a single company lies in the field of television advertising.

A big company can afford to advertise on television, and a small company cannot. A big company can afford the ten thousand dollars it costs for thirty seconds of prime time on a television network. It can afford the hundred thousand dollars it costs for ten such advertising spots. It can afford the million dollars it costs for a hundred of them. It can afford the millions of dollars it costs for the commercials it makes to go in them.

A small company can afford none of this. It can put up a sign outside the shop, a sign on the top of a parked car nearby; it can advertise now and then in the local suburban paper and once a year, maybe, in the Yellow Pages. But it can't engage in television advertising, and the big national market.

There are several results of this.

One is, obviously, that the big companies get customers that the small companies may deserve. Coca Cola is a good example of this: a somewhat addictive soft drink of no particular aesthetic distinction which, because of television advertising, seduces most of the youth of most of the nations of the world into its customer base. Hollywood, too, whose product, however mediocre, always outsells the better European, Australian or Asian films. And Cadbury's chocolate, and so on.

Another result is that the big companies are able to buy out the small companies and so suppress the better product and promote the worse. Small airlines, like Australia's Compass Airways, usually suffer in this way; so, everywhere in the world, do small publishing companies, small confectionery companies, small biscuit companies like Arnott's, small inventors, small tourist operators, and so on.

93

Apart from this, it is bloody annoying.

It is exactly the same as a performance on stage of *King Lear* or *La Traviata* being interrupted by a fire truck and men with axes and hoses and fire extinguishers on a night when there is no fire, and a man on a tannoy announcing that fire brigades as a generality are good for you.

We would not put up with it in the theatre. We would not put up with it in the cinema. Yet somehow we put up with it in the living room.

It is a ghastly unwelcome intrusion and should be banned on those grounds alone.

But there are, of course, additional grounds.

94

One of these is structural inflation.

For if thirty seconds of prime time costs ten thousand dollars, and thirty minutes costs six hundred thousand, and the advertisement itself costs two hundred thousand dollars to make (young men skateboarding off an aeroplane over the desert, or whatever), it's a cost the customer, eventually, will have to pay – an extra twelve cents for a can of Coke, an extra five thousand dollars for a Japanese car. This adds to inflation, which puts up the cost of everything, causes wage rises, more tax for those with, momentarily, higher wages, and so on.

It also erodes with interruptions the quality of television drama and, with minutes lost from every hour, the quality and thoroughness of television documentaries and news. For forty years the better television (*Z-Cars, I Claudius, The Singing Detective*) came from the BBC, which didn't have commercials, and the most contemptible (*Gunsmoke, Starsky and Hutch*) from CBS and NBC, which did. This meant a civilised, unviolent, thoughtful citizenry for the UK and a twitchy, frustrated, gun-waving mobocracy for the USA.

If there were no television commercials, and only newspaper advertisements and shop signs and some radio, prices would fall, and customers have a better choice of goods and services. On a *true* level playing field products would compete for customers on the basis of product quality, not Orwellian sales pitch. Local soft drinks, local biscuits, local cheeses, local beers, local shoes and hats and radios would have a chance.

Quality would count. *And competition actually take place.*

But not in a globalised economy.

There, because of television, the big automatically prevail, and the small have to struggle to be noticed.

So economic rationalism hurts, and often mortally hurts, small business.

And therefore abolishes competition.

Keep that in mind.

95

The true dishonourable end of economic rationalism (I suspect) is companies with economies that are bigger than whole countries, with factories in certain countries only – countries whose level of unemployment is so great that wages can be driven down and down, so that prices can be driven down and down, and the competition exterminated (on a level playing field) in the countries where the customers still have enough money to buy things.

96

These megacompanies, of course, have historical precedents – and the precedents are not just the British East India Company, a private company that between the years 1612 and 1813 ran an entire subcontinent, or the big British companies Drake and Hawkins worked for as privateers, attacking and boarding foreign ships and carrying off their gold and treasure and pretty girls, and sacking and burning foreign towns. There were other precedents, much bigger than that.

They were called Empires.

97

Like the modern global corporation, an Empire would seize land and minerals from a subject nation or buy them up cheap, then underpay a local workforce – the coolies who picked the coffee beans of Burma, the Zulus who worked the diamond mines of South Africa – for the products they would sell at a mighty profit in the motherlands of Belgium or France or Britain. When notions of equality, democracy and fair dealing grew and flourished in those subject nations, and the cost of labour grew too high, the imperial powers got out of them and left behind (as in most of Africa) a bloodstained confusion of misdrawn borders, tribal ferocities and tyrant chieftains with ancient grudges that haunt the former colonies to this day.

Global economics is a simple rerun of this process in most of the countries (Vietnam, China, Australia, Argentina) the Empires have left behind; and it takes the equivalent of Revolution to get rid of it, or to lessen the extent of its enslavement of peoples twice victims of this imperial process.

Hold onto that thought.

And tremble, while you are at it, with fear.

98

At some point the moral argument must at least be thought through. Whether it is *right* that some people born rich, or made rich by market manipulations, should be permitted to enslave other people born poor, or made poor by market manipulations, and demean their lives with unfit workplaces and unsafe conditions (this is tedious Marxist vituperation I know, but so is *The Simpsons*), and soil and corrode their destinies with suddenly abandoned traditions of work, or factory closures, or relocations of industries offshore. Or all of the above.

Or whether it is *wrong*.

If it is permissible for human beings to harass and

humiliate and ruin other human beings in the name of profit, and do so without let or fine or hindrance, then it is not a democratic system we are talking of, it is a tyranny.

99

Ergo, global economics is a sly and growing tyranny – much like older models – conceived without mercy and mostly unhindered, except in stiffnecked places familiar with bloodstained ravenous tyrannies and not too keen on them, like the European Union.

Most western governments suggest we go along with it, because there is no alternative.

100

'Each one hopes,' Winston Churchill said of those collaborationist governments like Vichy that came to terms with Hitlerism, 'each one hopes that if he feeds the crocodile enough, the crocodile will eat him last.'

Hitlerism was a former ravenous tyranny, and global economics shares its ambition, discuss. An ambition involving world conquest, slavery and great riches, discuss.

And slavery is not a good thing.

And a crocodile an unreliable business partner when he is hungry.

101

Hitlerism's worst discovery, probably, was that people are replaceable. That there are, in the end, always more desperate slaves, or inmates, ready to betray and bury their predecessors in return for their daily supply of just enough to eat.

It is an insight that global economics shares.

It is the most economically rational insight there is.

Follow the thread

102

It is worth, perhaps, looking back at what has been thus far said.

That economic rationalism as a theory lacks logic, and globalisation as currently practised is cruel – whether deliberately cruel or not has yet to be established. (As if that matters: the effect is cruel, anyway, and not to be borne.)

Economic rationalism, moreover, is not a new theory. It has its roots in slavery and Empire and (as John Ralston Saul established in *The Unconscious Civilization*) Mussolini's fascism. It changes its name and salespitch and protective colouring (this year it calls itself a 'more flexible workplace', or a 'freeing up of the marketplace', or a 'casting-off of the outdated shackles of union power'), but throughout this century and the last it has always come back, and always exploited and punished the many, and enriched and gratified the few, and touted the theory as a universal benefit for everybody.

Let us look a few more times at the theory, and how successful it has been through the present century.

Let us look – for a change of pace – at how economic rationalism, in a recent incarnation, affected, for argument's sake, the practice of sexual intercourse and procreation.

103

In the early twentieth century contraceptive devices and medical advance made possible the downsizing of families. Instead of twelve to fifteen children, three or four of whom died in infancy, parents could plan to have only four or five, none of whom need die young unless they were male and conscripted for service in war. This could be achieved with the use of condoms or, less reliably, the rhythm method.

And so it came to pass. By the mid-1920s, the average size in the West of the average Protestant family was four or five children, plus two parents. By the mid-1950s, it was three or four. By the mid-1970s, it was two or three. By the mid-1990s, fewer than two.

Because having fewer children, it was argued, would mean there would be more money earned by the family's breadwinner for each of its members and increased happiness would result. Children need not be crowded three or four to a room, and each could go on to college, if they were smart enough, and not be sent out to work at fourteen or fifteen, and not need to wear, with shame, the threadbare hand-me-down garments of their elder siblings.

Housing, moreover, would be cheaper because fewer children would need fewer rooms. Entertainment would be cheaper because fewer children would need fewer theatre tickets and fewer Chinese meals. Likewise fewer dental bills, because fewer teeth. Family holidays would be cheaper because fewer children would need fewer rail tickets and fewer rides on merry-go-rounds. All the guiding principles of economic rationalism were in place, to ensure greater happiness for everyone.

But . . . it didn't, or didn't entirely, turn out that way. There were hitches.

And by the century's end the price of housing had tripled, and a three-bedroom house cost twice what a five-bedroom house had cost, before inflation, in 1920. Whereas in 1920 one breadwinner brought home enough to keep in frugal comfort a family of five, by 1990 two breadwinners were needed to keep in quarrelsome poverty a family of three.

Affordable houses were smaller, backyards tiny, electrical bills and water rates twice what they were, dental bills four times what they were, train fares enormous, plane fares impossible, holidays unthinkable, exchange rates abominable and divorce everywhere. There was juvenile crime, drug abuse, youth suicide, and a sharp rise in domestic murder. In greater and greater numbers the children ran away and never came back.

And the experiment, moreover, had failed. For all the usual reasons. More trouble is caused (or nearly always caused) by adjusting the numbers than by leaving them alone.

104

What happened was this.

Dentists, finding fewer teeth to drill, put up their prices; and builders with fewer rooms to build did likewise. Houses, moreover, were not very often built because the 2.3 children to each family, when grown to adulthood, could mostly buy the old ones, after the death of their incumbents or their removal to retirement villages. This made house builders frantic, and they drove up their prices to make up for the months each year they were not at work, and this drove up the prices – still cheaper than the new ones – of existing houses, so that by 1992, forty-two percent of the average household income went into paying them off, as opposed to twenty-three percent in 1947.

This meant there was less disposable family income, fewer nights at the cinema, less buying of shirts and hats and shoes, and because there were fewer children, fewer shoes made, and the corner shoe repairman faded out of history. Because there were fewer customers (first abolish the customer) prices everywhere went up to meet investments, and inflation became a permanent feature of most economies. Fewer holidays up the coast, as well, and more need to attract tourists and Japanese investment and big hotels. Less activity in the economy and more need to talk up shares, and talk them down, in booms and busts that became a pattern.

105

Inflation is a by-product of contraception, discuss.

That was a joke.

106

House prices will go up to consume disposable income, discuss.

That is a numerical principle.

Whatever savings are made on the prices of smaller goods, the price of houses and the rent of houses will always go up to consume the difference.

Prove that I lie.

For a roof is the one thing you cannot do without, and will, if you are employed, pay anything for.

Prove that I lie.

And the argument that smaller families mean cheaper housing is fallacious.

107

And fewer children also meant fewer schoolchildren, after the Baby Boom generation, and fewer schools and fewer schoolteachers, who were sacked and laid off in their hundreds of thousands, and so deprived of the first step of a career path of so many eminent citizens. And there was less government money for state schools because their populations had shrunk, and more selling off of old school buildings by governments fond of privatisation and seizing their big chance.

Real estate became the preoccupation of a whole generation, and family fortunes made and lost with its manipulations.

'They call it real estate,' became the cry, 'because it's *real.* It can't get up and walk away.' And money tied up in it was never used in more creative ways. Whole skyscrapers were built and left empty for want of people to fill them, because they had not, alas, thanks to contraceptive rationalism, been born.

And then, of course, there is the social cost.

108

The children of small families have found themselves under increasing pressure – from parents who vest in them all their hopes.

When there were five sons and three daughters, any one of them – or any three – could do badly at school, or be sacked from their initial jobs, and the parents would wear it, because there were more where they came from, who would perhaps do well in the world, and gratify their old father.

But now when there is usually only one son, he has no option but to become President of the United States or Prime Minister of Australia, or top of the class, or a football star, or a swimming champion, or a computer billionaire.

And if there are two daughters and no sons, one of them has to fulfil the role, or the career path, of a son, or something like it.

They may not do this, of course. But when they do not the family tension rises, and the pressure builds, and the child may opt out of the whole process, and take drugs, or run away, or suicide, as teenagers increasingly do, on the eve of threatening exams. In cultures where high academic performance is most prized, like Japan or the southern counties of England, the family misery is greatest. Stories are told, apocryphal perhaps, of Japanese mothers sexually servicing their only sons in order to ease their emotional tension during exams.

And if there are two children and one of them is accidentally killed, or dies of leukaemia, the effect on the parents is emotionally catastrophic. (The author is one of three children, one of whom was killed, and can testify to this.) Whereas if there are six children, the family can, and will, go on.

109

It is probable, though not certain, that the fashion for smaller families is the prime cause of the modern upsurge in divorce.

Part of it is situational. A mother of one child may consider taking a job, whereas a mother of six children will not. A woman spending time away from the home environment may consider adultery. A woman ill-treated or underestimated in the home environment may consider taking the one child and leaving. A mother of six children will rarely do that. She is too preoccupied with the intricate enormities of love.

But part of it is emotional. A large family, however ill-accommodated, is a pleasing unit with built-in alliances and parlour games and secret languages, home help and babysitting, training for social discourse and compromise and parenthood and partnership – and most products of such families remember the past with fondness, and cannot imagine growing up in any other way. If told by the politically correct they would have been happier if there had been four fewer of them, they react with bewildered amazement. They know that this is not so.

If it were so, then three quarters of the Irish should have been aborted, in order to make that society a happier one.

I am glad they were not, because I have met them, or some of them, and their society is among the happiest on earth.

110

Because having sixteen uncles and aunts and a hundred cousins gives you a lot of room to move in, a lot of intimates to confide in, a lot of couches to sleep on, a lot of Christmas gatherings to revel in, a lot of songs to sing, the way the Irish do. It is like a miniature welfare state, with available care for everyone, because blood tells.

111

Having only one child, however, the way, in modern times, the Chinese do – and must, for their society prescribes, and their government enforces, one child per family – raises problems.

The first is whether or not to murder the baby if it is a girl.

(It is economically rational to murder a baby if it is a girl. Girls in China over a lifetime earn less money.)

The next is how to get over the grief of having murdered the little girl.

The next is how to avoid spoiling the one child you do have, a child without aunties or siblings or cousins, and how to acclimatise him to society and find him playmates.

The next is what to do about the roving gangs of young Chinese men unable to get women because not enough women, when born, were allowed to survive their birth, young men very sexually frustrated now, and what to do about the young women they chase down alleys and gang-rape.

It's rational all right, but it's also crazy.

112

The argument need not be overstressed. But it is clear that the bland assertion that smaller families have more fun, or are in some overall sense happier families, or more viable social units, has tremendous logical flaws.

Yet this is precisely the way an economic rationalist thinks. Eliminate the superfluous. Maximise the output of the smaller number. Cut the operation back to the bone.

There are many weeping Chinese women, weeping and going mad because they followed these earnest arithmetical precepts.

And many Irish mothers being sung to by great gatherings of their children and grandchildren because they did not.

113

It might be argued that unless we all have even fewer children than we do now the exhausted planet will come to an end, but I doubt it. The entire present population of the world (or so I am informed) could be accommodated standing up on the Isle of Wight, and the sea is a most unexploited source of energy and food and living space, and two big pipes could probably revivify Australia's Inland Sea and change its ecosystem, and so on. It is not beyond the wit of humankind to build whole mountain ranges and attract snow with them and make new rivers and so on. (Stop me if you've heard these things.)

And if there is not enough food there will be famines and plagues and tribal wars like those in Ruanda, and billions will die, but they will in the meantime have *lived*, and their parents before them, and their parents before them.

It is a dreadful thing to suggest that it would be better if none of the above had ever been born. That three quarters, or five sixths, of the Irish should never have been born.

I do not believe it.

That James Joyce, one of ten children, should never have been born.

I do not believe it.

The population-reduction argument is an economic rationalist one.

I do not believe it.

First abolish the customer.

I do not believe it.

114

One of the most straightforward arguments for big families is that when you are widowed and old you can go and stay for two months of each year with each of your six children and their families, and they will look after you. You can acquaint yourself with your grandchildren, and then move on to another set of grandchildren, through a happy old age.

But . . . if you have only one child he will not look after you all year round.

He will imprison you in a nursing home and leave you there to go mad. His time is valuable. He, moreover, has been spoiled and thinks only of himself.

He doesn't need you.

This is not to say that sixteen children is not too many.

But it is to say that one is probably too few.

Find me one mother with seven children who regrets having had the final six.

Find me just one.

And if you cannot, then tell me what your arguments are that she would be happier without them.

115

Another historic example of economic anorexia can be found in the live theatre. Once self-supporting, it is now, thanks to an early outbreak of economic rationalism, everywhere pretty well a basket case, and in grave need of government subsidy.

By the start of the twentieth century, all forms of theatre, from music hall to the intellectual comedies and dramas of George Bernard Shaw and Wilde and Pinero, were so popular as to be self-supporting. Their casts rarely numbered fewer than ten, and theatre managements commonly employed as many as fifty-five or sixty people – on stage, in the dressing room, collecting the tickets, tending the bar and cloakroom, changing the sets, working the lights, and conducting and playing incidental music in the orchestra pit. The length of most dramas – and nearly all musicals – exceeded three hours and afforded a fair deal of time, during two fifteen-minute intervals, for a fair deal of money to be made from the consumption of sandwiches and whisky and icecream and chocolates in the upstairs and downstairs bars.

By the 1940s however, in part as a result of the determined competition of the then palatial cinemas, whose ticket prices were lower and star performers better known, the live theatre industry began, the way one does, to downsize.

People were sacked from all parts of the building.

Ticket sellers doubled as bar-tenders. Scene shifters doubled as make-up assistants and minor actors. Lighting systems became automated, and atmospheric music pre-recorded.

Cast sizes, moreover, came down. In place of the two hundred professional performers required by (for instance) Noel Coward's *Cavalcade*, there was a cast of only seven for Noel Coward's *Blithe Spirit*. Plays with a broad canvas, therefore, involving the fate of nations and the murder of monarchs, regular features of the theatre since its Athenian beginnings, became impossible to mount. Plays involving seven people and an unchanging set with cocktail cabinets and French windows, many of them arch and tedious comedies, became the staple of Shaftesbury Avenue and Broadway.

And at the same time it became clear to the numbers men that if the bar staff were sent home early you would not have to pay them overtime. Theatre managements therefore let it be known that plays with two acts, and therefore only one interval, would be welcomed, and three-act dramas greeted with suspicion.

This meant plays of the J.B. Priestley and Peter Ustinov sort, where Act One is in 1914, Act Two in 1939 and Act Three in 1960, would no longer be considered and were therefore no longer written. And so by 1960 the number of theatre workers, front and backstage, had fallen from an average population of sixty to an average population of eighteen.

But worse was to come.

Its name was Harold Pinter.

116

Pinter proved you could keep a theatre audience in a semi-comatose condition of stupefied reverence with a play employing only three actors, a good deal of repetitiveness and no discernible exposition, and with it achieve the cautious admiration of critics and those large gatherings of snobs who applauded and followed the vagaries of their taste.

Three actors, then, and two perchance, became the required goal of managements – preferably star players.

And so, with some exceptions, it came to pass: a tradition of drama, invented by economic rationalism, involving only two or three actors who stood on the one set hinting at Everything.

117

The numbers added up, of course, but the audience numbers kept mysteriously falling. Soon it became widely agreed that no theatre could survive anymore without taxpayer subsidy. Political action began, and subsidy was achieved, and large bureaucracies set up to administer it. The only exceptions to this economic inevitability seemed to be those revivals of big

Broadway musicals – *South Pacific, Guys and Dolls, The King and I* – which made money despite their many actors, lavish costumes, costly stage machinery, thirty-piece orchestras, and expensive tickets. Audiences inexplicably preferred to pay big money for what they regarded as (oh yes) their money's worth.

And so the situation, thanks to economic rationalism, remains today: on the one hand a subsidised theatre of swelling snobbery that nightly plays to a shrivelling audience of educated social climbers, and on the other hand a commercial theatre like that of the 1890s that easily makes money out of large casts, dazzling theatre effects and big noisy orchestras.

118

And the explanation for this anomaly – apart from the audience's desire to get its money's worth – may go something like this.

All human beings have relatives and many have loyal, caring friends. A play with thirty actors in it, therefore, will attract perhaps two hundred of the actors' relatives and friends who then, if the play is any good, will begin to speak in its praise to other acquaintances.

The choreographers, musicians and set designers, the ticket collectors and backstage workers, the cloakroom attendants and icecream sellers, will also have relatives and friends. This may add up to a basic loyal audience of a thousand people, and a box-office income, in the early weeks, of fifty thousand dollars. This will allow the management the cost of larger display advertisements and television spots. It will boost the actors' morale. It will increase the electricity of the performance, as the audiences grow and grow.

This is rarely the case with a cast of three – who, more often than not, dislike each other – and an uncrowded dressing room after the performance bereft of affectionate jollity, relatives, agents and popping champagne.

As a result, therefore, of economic rationalism the unsubsidised live theatre is dying. Its fate is similar to all those other private enterprises that read the numbers but cannot interpret what they actually mean.

119

Another example.

In more recent times it was decided that the buses of Sydney should no longer have conductors because you had to pay the conductors, and the driver should collect the tickets as well as drive the bus. Thus the wage bill of each journey was nearly halved.

But . . . the time it took for the driver to sell the tickets and give change meant the journey now took thirty percent longer than it used to. So there were fewer bus journeys, and in order to make up the numbers more bus drivers had to be hired, and more buses bought.

And people, noting how long the bus journeys now took, began to travel less often by that mode of transport.

And old women, moreover, and younger women too, felt less safe than they used to, without a conductor, especially at night. And they started travelling less at those hours, and business fell off.

And the number of buses travelling was therefore reduced and sold off to hippies as dwellings. And people waited longer and longer between buses, and spent longer and longer on them.

And the government became unpopular and lost office.

And very little money was saved.

120

An even more moronic thing was done with trains – by a man called Greiner, who had a degree in economics from Harvard and was for a time, alas, the Premier of New South Wales.

Trains used to travel overnight from the state capital, Sydney, to Australia's favourite tourist resort, the Gold Coast. There were sleeping cars on the trains, with double compartments for couples or family groups, and single roomettes for people travelling alone. Both sorts of sleeper had toilets in them, and the double compartments had private showers. There was also a dining car where you could dine at night, drink wine, observe the darkening scenery and breakfast watching the sunrise.

You could take your car on the train, and drive it off at journey's end and continue on your way through the Gold Coast.

The train left at 6 or 6.30 at night, and arrived at the Gold Coast at 10 or 10.30 a.m. the following day. You arrived refreshed and showered and breakfasted and energetic, ready for your holiday. A steward awoke you with a cup of tea and a biscuit at whatever hour you chose to come to.

Greiner found all this extravagant and wasteful, and determined to improve things.

If there were *faster* trains and fewer people working on them, he argued, the railways would make a profit, whereas now (in part because of the many old people who travelled free) they were losing money.

So he downsized, rationalised and sped things up.

He sacked a third of the staff, including the tea-and-biscuit providers, and the chefs and waiters of the dining car.

He replaced the dining car with a buffet that sold fast food and light beer and peanuts and chocolates.

The buffet occupied only half a car, and the food was terrible.

He sold off all the sleeping cars. Why do people need to sleep? More people, moreover, could be accommodated sitting up.

(By the same logic, hotels without beds could accommodate more people, if only they could be taught to sleep standing up.)

He sold off all the sleeping cars, which everybody loved, for about three thousand dollars each. He sold off the platform carriages that the motorists used to put their cars on. No-one could take their cars any-more. That was wasteful and extravagant. And he got a whole new kind of train.

This train went faster, and shook a lot, and if it left Sydney at 4.20 p.m. (an hour before the customer gets off work) it arrived at Casino, on the lower Gold Coast not at 6.30 a.m. as it used to, but at 3.20 a.m. People staggered out at 3.20 a.m. aghast and looking for taxis, and there weren't any.

They didn't have their cars anymore, and they missed them.

And those who wished to go to Byron Bay had to get on a bus.

This was inconvenient, and cramped, and frequently stopping, and an enemy of sleep. It was afflicted too by a bus driver who believed himself a stand-up comedian and in the pre-dawn hours told bad jokes loudly over the intercom.

The traveller arrived at Byron Bay at 6.30 a.m. an emotional ruin and, having slept for the whole day, woke up at midnight like one jetlagged with nothing to do.

The people started to complain that they wanted the sleepers back.

At great expense, having sold off the sleepers, the fool had a whole new kind of sleeper designed. It had glass walls, and curtains and a toilet-and-shower between compartments.

To go to the toilet at night you had to rise, draw the curtain, dress, go out into the corridor, enter the toilet, come back again, undress, and climb a swaying ladder back into bed.

Old people who had to go five times a night found this a trial.

Moreover, because the train was going much faster

you couldn't sleep at all. You were flung about like one caught in a cement mixer.

And there were no single compartments. You were stuck with whatever snoring and farting Scientologist you were coupled with.

People stopped travelling by train.

They hated it.

As a result of this fewer people visited country towns, whose economies declined. Fewer people stayed at tourist motels. It was too much trouble. And more people, driving, died in road accidents on the shabby highways.

By this means Greiner saved maybe fifty million dollars in the first year, then less each year as the rail service grew more repellent to its users. In the meantime, probably no more than forty extra people died on the roads.

In Queensland, meanwhile, a luxury train modelled on the Orient Express, with dining car, club car, gourmet food and plush compartments, started making profits.

Economic anorexia here, economic gluttony there.

And guess which won, and kept its customer base, and so prevailed.

That's right.

121

At the heart of Greiner's lunacy was his belief, shared by many of his fellow rationalists, that time is only time. And the more you save of it, the more you have to spend in other ways.

But to arrive early in Casino, and so lose the emotional and spiritual benefit of a full night's sleep, saves you a couple of hours of travel but – in tiredness, bad temper and jangled neurasthenia – costs you a day of pleasure.

It is better for you, and more *economical*, in short, to arrive at 6.30 a.m. not 3.30 a.m., at Casino station, or at 8.10 a.m. at Byron Bay refreshed and energetic and have the day in its fullness.

Time is well used, or not well used. It is never saved, discuss.

122

A shorter, sadder example of the lunacy of this cost-saving tendency occurred at the end of World War I.

The light horse brigades that had won Beersheba (in the last great cavalry charge of history) and taken Damascus ahead of Lawrence of Arabia, and had been, overall, the best and bravest soldiers in the Middle East, were told that, *in view of the limited space on returning troopships,* they would have to shoot their horses before sailing home.

These were horses from their own farms in Western Australia, horses they had trained, with, sailed with, fought with, slept beside, and won their battles with. They had been their companions, fellow warriors and friends. And now they had to personally shoot them through the head.

Just to avoid the expense of bringing to the Mediterranean another couple of troopships to take the horses home.

The men complied, and some, as late as 1998, were still grieving for the friends they were told to kill.

It made a mockery of their valour and a bad joke of their victory. It made them curse their country. It traumatised them like the death of human friends. It haunted their manhood and middle age. It made them feel like criminals, Judases, murderers, fratricides.

And it saved, maybe, some twenty thousand pounds in the chartering of troopships.

The horses had names, and were friends.

Don't think about it. Don't think about it anymore.

123

All saving has a human cost, discuss.

124

A human equivalent of the equine massacre recounted above may be found in the Irish Potato Famine.

A vegetable microbe, *phytophthora infestans*, attacked and destroyed the potatoes of Ireland in 1845. The Irish peasantry, subjects of English and Anglo-Irish landlords and at work, in the main, as tenant farmers on their estates, were thus deprived of their usual sustenance. They began to starve – children, women, babies – in great numbers.

The men who harvested wheat and corn for English landlords, and sought to take some home to feed their children, were kept away from it at gunpoint. As thousands and then tens of thousands died, an appeal was made to the English government for permission to eat what could be eaten and pay for it later.

The English government thought it best not to interfere in the free workings of the market.

Whole families died, emaciated in their mud-and-straw accommodations. Starving fathers were shot while stealing food for their starving children.

Money was sent from Australasia, the United States and Canada, and some of it got through. The workhouses of the coastal towns filled up with orphan children. Soon schemes were contrived by charitable groups to export the children and able-bodied adults to Boston, and Sydney, and Wellington, and the great migration began.

By 1850 two million Irish had gone overseas – among them Kennedys and Reagans and Healeys and Keatings and Richardsons and Breretons and Faheys and McClellands and Bourkes and Gairs and Chifleys, and Daleys and Youngs and Langs and Lawrences and Cullens, and the parents, of course, of Ned Kelly, and so it goes – to recreate their culture and sing their songs of home in places far from the bays and bogs and green hills and misty distances they loved and always remembered.

And one million out of nine million Irish died. Because it was not economically rational to feed them with the food that was there to eat.

And for a hundred and fifty years thereafter the sons and grandsons of the dispossessed and sacrificed bought guns and built bombs and planned assassinations and carried them out. Why wouldn't they? And London became for decades an intermittent battleground and a tourism debacle, and young men starved themselves to death in gaol and Margaret Thatcher sent out hit squads to kill IRA 'suspects' and the IRA retaliated by blowing up a hotel containing her cabinet, and so it went.

And what a profit margin there was.

Free trade had to be preserved. And the Irish peasantry were expendable.

Expendable as Kleenex.

125

This lack of a moral component in economic rationalism – the belief that only the figures mean anything, and only the bottom line matters, and the human cost is beyond accountancy – may not be as big a question as its logical stupidity, and the other thing of which we must not speak – or not speak yet – but it has importance.

For a belief in numbers only can easily justify the heroin trade. And the marketing by Nestlé in Third World countries of the powdered milk formula that killed so many babies. And the British trade in land mines that killed and mutilated so many children. And the marketing into whoredom of little girls who die of AIDS.

If only the numbers matter, then people do not matter, discuss.

126

The heroin trade fits into the rational-imperial model very well indeed. As in the British Empire,

Asian peasants grow the base crop very cheaply. It is transported, treated, mixed with powdered milk, and sold to eager customers in the large imperialist countries at a huge profit, sometimes ten thousand percent. These customers are very happy to receive it. Ecstatic in fact.

As in the best economic rationalist models, there is no tax on the manufacture and sale. Just as the academic theorists would wish, it competes on a level playing field with beer, chocolate, champagne and fairy floss, and wins hands down, and achieves a loyal customer base. As they would wish there is little government interference in the freedom of its trade, or little that matters. It takes place within metres of police stations, in broad daylight, and is mostly not hindered.

But . . . heroin ruins lives, and ends many. It drains away life's meaning from the parents and siblings and spouses of the eager customers. It is a direct cause of burglaries, and muggings and the armed robbery of banks and service stations, and of AIDS from dirty needles, and of AIDS and smack addictions in prisons, and deaths from Ecstasy at rave parties, and suicides in prison, and executions by hanging of addicted couriers by hypocritical Asian governments, and the alienation of youth from their society, and the corruption of police, and the rising costs of insurance premiums for policies relating to burglaries and house-breaking.

But . . . the brave entrepreneurs (and they *are* brave) make a lot of money. And the customers get the superior product they want. And that's all that matters. And the Board of Directors is delighted. The figures add up. And that's all that matters, isn't it?

The moral component is none of the entrepreneurs' concern.

The figures add up.

127

They add up too in the tobacco trade, or they used to. Crops are reaped – by slaves once, now by wage slaves – in depressed communities and children systematically addicted to a poison that, happily, may take forty years to kill them. So consuming is the addiction that the eager customers will pay almost any price to acquire the poison, despite bans on advertising and compulsory labelling that warns, now, of certain death. (The addiction is more widespread in Third World countries where there are fewer bans on advertising, and labelling that is less harsh, and more need because of poverty in the customers for a relaxing pastime.)

The customers get cancer, of course (first abolish

the customer), but they don't get it for a very long time, and in the meantime they buy lots of the product. Some of them are still smoking it on the day before they drown in their own blood. The author's father did this after two years of gasping and regret, and it's not a good way to go.

But the *bottom line* is magnificent, and that's the main thing.

128

But . . . of late a lot of dying people are suing, and the bottom line is altering.

A court case of lung-cancer sufferers against Philip Morris achieved a payment of 496 million dollars (and this was just in Florida and Miami) for medical costs, and the share price of Philip Morris is plummeting.

Maybe the moral component affects the bottom line after all.

Maybe the moral questions matter.

Maybe they make money.

129

If a government can make laws hindering the sale of heroin and tobacco merely because they ruin lives and sometimes end them, why – as a matter of philosophical debate – cannot they make laws that hinder the evils of economic rationalism? It also ruins lives, and ends them.

The EU does it.

What is the problem?

130

Some say tobacco and heroin are different, but they are not.

They are different only in that they ruin the lives of customers, and economic rationalism ruins the lives of employees, or former employees, and ends them. In both cases the customer is abolished.

131

How is this to be sorted out?

A fine, perhaps, of a hundred thousand dollars for every employee sacked by a multinational corporation, the money to go directly to the sackee, and three months in gaol for the sacker.

Maybe not. But it's a thought.

It's what happens in some countries to heroin dealers. And river polluters.

And corporation troubleshooters do as much harm as either. Don't they?

Keep this in mind when we get to the matter of which we must not speak.

A ghost in the machine

132

Fundamental to the heart, the frigid heart, of economic rationalism is a failure to understand how economies work.

They know *some* part of how they work, but they leave out, and treat as non-existent, some of the crucial ingredients.

Some are to do with customer loyalty. Some are to do with staff loyalty. Some are to do with aggressive creativity, the sort that happens with a worker long loyal, and identified with his company. Some are to do with unexpected inventions, and the climate that breeds invention. All are to do with imagination.

133

In the 1930s, for instance, Australian cameramen from Cinesound Newsreels were sent to England to cover the Test cricket, the famous Bodyline Tour of 1932, for instance, and film a little of the new batting marvel, young Don Bradman, as part of their work.

They were given eight minutes of film to cover a five-day Test.

This was economically rational. Film stock was expensive, and only two or three minutes, if that, would ever end up on screen.

'Get the wickets,' the cameramen were told. The result was a lot of shots of melancholy batsmen walking away from shattered stumps.

And so it was that the great innings of Sir Donald Bradman – his 334 at Leeds in 1930, his 304 at Leeds in 1934, his 238 at Lords in 1948 – were never put down on film.

Had this happened there would now be a fortune to be made by the newsreel owners from sports channels, biographical films, and CD-ROMs on the art of batting and how cricket has changed.

There would also be a documentary compilation called *Keith Miller Superstar* or *Gentlemen Players*, and others on Dennis Compton and Garfield Sobers and Wesley Hall and Freddy Trueman. The existential moment of crisis and the grace it brings would be there forever for generations unborn to find joy in and learn from.

But no, the film stock at five shillings per minute was too costly, and so a financial bonanza, and an educational miracle, was lost.

It was there to be had, and is no more – thanks to economic rationalism in an early incarnation.

And we have instead a few dozen shots of broken wickets, and heroes walking sadly away.

134

The Australian Broadcasting Commission, in a similar act of rationalism, decided in 1974 to clear its shelves of most of its old television broadcasts that were not in colour.

Thus it gained shelf space and avoided building an extra storage facility that would have cost, then, eight thousand pounds. And it got rid of tens of thousands of hours of black-and-white material that had no future.

All of its first drama series, *Stormy Petrel*, on Captain Bligh and John Macarthur, was thus destroyed. All of *Six O'Clock Rock*, compered by Australia's equivalent of Elvis, Johnny O'Keefe. The news bulletins that covered the Cuban crisis, the Kennedy assassination, the drowning of Prime Minister Holt. Destroyed rather than given away to television aficionados and history scholars, who would have taken it gladly – because giving it away was illegal. It was government property.

Much of it was pulped, and the celluloid mash

thus created used in the manufacture of automobile polish. The figures are not available but it is probable that each can of film thus mulched earned the ABC two dollars.

This lost material, this precious lost cultural history, would needless to say have made money, and lots of money, on the cable television channels of today – on TV1 or Arena or TNT – and would have brought amusement at different levels to new generations as *I Love Lucy* has, and *The Naked City*, and *The Honeymooners*, and *The Twilight Zone*, to sleepless people and shiftworkers and babysitters and cat burglars across the modern world.

But shelf space was saved. And a little money made from a car-polish factory.

And that was economically rational.

135

Had Van Gogh's brother Theo been as foresighted as the men from the ABC, he would have told his unstable sibling that if he didn't sell five paintings in the next six months he would cut off his money and force him into some other line of work, or beggary, or portrait sketching on the streets. Thus Van Gogh would have been 'encouraged' to paint properly. And live therefore like a rational man.

As it happened Theo loved his brother and kept supporting him. And Van Gogh did not sell a painting in his lifetime.

But Alan Bond bought one, in 1984, for twenty-five million dollars.

136

In 1646, likewise, a wealthy fowl-breeder in Stratford-Upon-Avon bought a large house called New Place, the previous residence of William Shakespeare, the actor and playwright.

He searched the house and found in it a room full of papers in Shakespeare's handwriting, scripts and personal letters signed by the dead householder.

He decided to use the room to breed pheasants in, and so took all the papers out into the courtyard and burned them in a pile. It took perhaps three hours to do this.

By this classic rationalist decision he was able to use his asset profitably, and breed many pheasants which he then sold to local aristocrats fond of shooting them.

But . . . the burnt letters, *pensées*, direction notes, complaints to actors, joke verses, first drafts and unfinished dramas would by now by valued in the hundreds of millions, and be a boon and a treasure trove to academics, historians, play directors, modern performers and drama teachers the world over.

He did the rational thing, however, and the ashes of lost magic floated up and over the Avon Valley, and then were seen no more.

And he made a tidy profit engendering and selling beautiful doomed birds.

The way an economic rationalist would.

137

A tired old Oscar Wilde line about cynics applies to economic rationalists: they know the price of everything and the value of nothing.

138

For the price of things varies – does it not? – through time.

After President Kennedy was shot and his life upgraded into bright legend his grieving fans paid money in great amounts for moulds of his feet, clippings of his hair, the rocking chair he sat in, the machine that kept on signing his name to thank-you letters for three days after he died. Documentary film of him at work in the White House became a treasure trove for television historians and conspiracy theoreticians. Tens of millions of dollars were made from books that guessed who his murderers were; or interviewed his many sexual partners – Audrey Hepburn, Angie Dickinson, Grace Kelly, Judith Exner; or pondered his role in the death of Marilyn Monroe.

These millions would never have been made had history been different, or the third bullet missed him, as it might have.

Millions came out of nowhere, because of an event, because of an idea.

139

And it is this very interesting fact that money can be *created,* out of an event, or an idea, or an accident – like the one that ended the life of Princess Diana – that has eluded the economically correct.

That a dead film star like James Dean can become an industry. That a song by Bob Dylan, or a book by Ralph Nader, or a book by Germaine Greer, or a book by Marshall McLuhan, can alter the priorities of human lives and therefore a nation's economy. That a series of paintings by Andrew Wyeth of his overweight Swedish housemaid nude in afternoon light can for largely unverbalisable reasons become a bestselling picturebook. That any piece of writing, however workaday (a radio script of no interest, a film script still unfinished) by Dylan Thomas now has market value. And money comes almost from nowhere to buy it.

There is an X-factor, therefore, in economics that the rationalists have not picked up.

A ghost in the machine.

140

Picasso, for instance, had friends who were often down on their luck. And he would meet them at his usual cafe and in less than a minute do a lightning sketch on a little pad, *and sign it,* and give it to them. And such was the value of the *signature* that his paupered friends could eat for a month after selling the sketch to a tourist.

It was like magic somehow. It was amazing.

It was voodoo economics.

Voodoo economics that worked.

141

A similar kind of voodoo is created by music.

'How strange it is,' Shakespeare said, 'that sheep's guts can hale men's souls out of their bodies.'

And the tune of *Danny Boy* can still make money – for orchestras, for singers – a thousand years after it was written.

142

But how is this magic spell created? This angelic force that summons money out of nowhere? Where does it come from? How is it constituted?

Take an example.

143

In 1965 in Britain a university drop-out and a solicitor's clerk wrote a short musical entertainment for school children to enact which delighted the children's parents when they produced it in the school hall. It was called *Joseph and His Amazing Technicolor Dreamcoat*, and the encouragement the two young men got from it fuelled a further project, and it came in stages. First, there were just six notes – composed, as it happened, by Mozart – and a title *Jesus Christ Superstar* – a title brilliant in its banality, all agreed – and then the completed song. Then there were other songs, and an album. The album became a concert. The concert became a show.

The show straddled the two prevailing currents of belief in the West in the 1960s, conventional Christianity and the new youth freedom, powered by the Pill, marijuana and a restless, roving sexual rapacity.

The show became a dozen productions, a Hollywood film, a hundred productions, a thousand. It spawned star careers in the theatre for directors, arrangers, lead singers, designers. On its back new theatres were built, and new theatre districts; new expensive shows were mounted, and new recording companies and film companies launched. The primacy of Broadway in musicals was broken, and restored after seventy years to England.

The two authors wrote other shows, together and apart, and became multimillionaires. Both eventually were knighted. Sir Tim Rice and Sir Andrew Lloyd Webber, now Lord Webber. Sir Andrew's relatives became famous, with albums of their own. A minor political figure, Eva Peron, became world famous and revered. A low-selling poet, T.S. Eliot, achieved pop superstardom like the Christ.

Where had all this money *come* from?

Once there were two young men, two words and six notes . . .

Well, first, it came from taxpayer subsidies for the courses in composition and orchestration Lord Webber took at Guildhall and the Royal College of Music. On top of this was a further subsidy, from his loyal father who staked his efforts to avoid academe and become a composer. And then there was the free use he had of thirty-eight choirboys and a rundown school hall and a single piano: free inspiring tools of his trade he could not, at market prices, have otherwise afforded, free advantages to work with and learn from.

And it came, of course, from a man who carried a cross up a hill once and was nailed to it, and the nineteen hundred years of pre-publicity attendant on his high and holy name and bloodstained execution. It came from the turmoil his movement had been in for the hundred years since Darwinism and archaeology conspired to bring into question his belief system, and the eleven years since a man-made satellite with a dog in it and bigger and bigger telescopes had searched the skies and found no sign of heaven.

It came from the new upsurge of British music, powered by The Beatles and The Rolling Stones and the new strain of cantankerous, questioning songs, popularised by Bob Dylan, which attacked and examined and sneered at the tenets of western Christian society. It came from the piano lessons that the baby Mozart got from his unrelenting father.

It came from a lot of things. It did not come from nowhere. It did not come, as economic rationalism does, from a moral vacuum with numbers written on it.

It came, moreover, from the power of music, a power that cannot be measured or rationalised.

A ghost, as they say, in the machine.

144

An economic rationalist, nineties style, would not have put money into *Superstar* – and so lost his company billions.

'To portray Christ on stage,' he would have said, 'was *illegal* till 1967 and is still pretty dodgy today, in 1968. To do it in America will cause incensed fundamentalists to burn the theatre down. Blasphemy is still a crime in both countries, England and America, Squire. Drug arrests will occur backstage and deprive us of our lead on opening night. The reviews of the snob critics will be savage. It will close in a week.'

Economic rationalists think like that.

145

Because all they want to deal with, really, is what is already *there*.

They will buy an airline company and sack its ground crew and safety officers, and get its profits way, way up, and sell it off. But they would never subsidise Leonardo da Vinci for twenty years to dream that man may some day fly.

They will buy up the Apple Corporation and sell off its component songs to Michael Jackson for millions. But they would never have bought Paul McCartney his first guitar.

To have done that would have incurred a financial risk.

They only like things that are real, like real estate. They have no truck with dreams, with ghosts that might turn into fortunes, or might not.

146

An economic rationalist would have sacked Albert Einstein from Princeton when, after four years, he had not come up with his Field Theory of the Universe.

'Get rid of him,' the rationalist would have said, 'he has not come up with the goods, he is no longer earning his keep. Relativity was *years* back, where's his next big product? He hasn't *produced*, get rid of him.'

But . . . just *because* Einstein was famed and revered, and resident at Princeton (with his pencil and his notebook, thinking about things) a lot more kids enrolled at Princeton and its coffers grew. A lot of good academics went there too, because he was there, and the overall quality of the teaching staff improved. And because the quality was up, the fees could safely be raised, and the campus grew in prestige and *therefore* financial stability.

It happens like that. It's called Goodwill.

147

Goodwill exists. It's a legal concept; it has weight, validity and substance. It means, in law, the advantage that a company gets from a name, and such past approval as a man in the street will re-experience when reading or hearing that name.

Thus Bradman Cricket Supplies gives that shop an advantage, whereas Manson Cutlery does not. Lismore Cordials gives that company an advantage in Lismore, whereas Grafton Beer does not.

Goodwill is what, in the end, makes people trade. Economies exist because people trade, and not the other way around.

Ergo, Goodwill is the basis of an economy.

Then there is Badwill.

148

Badwill is why people do *not* trade, and economies therefore cease.

Badwill is why Telstra lost customers after they sacked twenty-five thousand of their employees, some of those customers relatives of the sackees, but not all. It was why Nestlé lost customers after selling, without a warning label, powdered milk to tens of thousands of Third World mothers whose babies became addicted to it, and when it became unaffordable died in great numbers. It is why nuclear power lost customers after Chernobyl radiated most of Europe and killed with leukaemia and bone cancer many Ukrainian children. It is why Air New Zealand suffered a profit drop when two hundred and seventy-five of its joyriders and air crew crashed into Mount Erebus in Antarctica. It is why boxing lost popularity after Muhammad Ali became a dim, slurred, shambling travesty of the sassy golden legend he once was. It was why baseball lost popularity when, in the twenties, its top team proved to be on the take. It is why Quintex lost market share after its founder, Christopher Skase, absconded with millions to Majorca and stayed there, putting on an oxygen mask and refusing to come home. It is why Bond University lost credibility, and paying students, when Alan Bond its founder went to gaol. It is why BHP lost credibility, and public support, and profit margin, after closing down its Newcastle Steelworks. People didn't like it.

Put it this way.

Everything quoted above lost profit margins, credibility, market share and goodwill because of economic rationalism. All made choices that *in the short run* increased profit margins – Nestlé by not printing a warning label and sticking it on, Muhammad Ali by taking one more million-dollar punch to the head – but *in the long run* lost them the goodwill that is, was, must be, the only way to prevail in the marketplace.

Thus, in an odd way – not always, but *eventually* – sales come hand in hand with good morality.

And the badwill that comes with rationalist practice kills the company that spawns it.

Good morality is good economics, discuss.

149

For the badwill does not just infect and pollute the customer base. It infects and pollutes and corrodes its own workforce as well.

John Ralston Saul in his remarkable book, *The Unconscious Civilization,* reports how employees who have narrowly survived the sack that extinguished their workmates and friends become, as a rule, very nervous, and haggard, and overworked, and *uncreative.*

They are uncreative because they fear making any suggestions whatever lest the New Broom sack them as he has sacked so many others. The New Broom has no experience of their line of work and he wants nothing unpredictable happening, thank you very much, he wants only to crunch costs down and profits up, way up.

They are tired because three hundred of them

now do the work of their five hundred predecessors. They are working seventy and eighty hours a week to keep up, seeing little of their children and wives and pub and golf companions and looking sideways, most nights, at those like-minded workmates who may (or may not) be plotting their exit also. And while this is happening to them, what is happening to the company is the erosion and disintegration of its corporate memory and its culture.

For many of those the New Broom so rudely extinguished were older employees, who took away with them much of the past that might have been useful: old pitfalls, old untried solutions, old slogans and war cries and sage words of general advice. And because no new apprentices are being taken on (under the econo-misers of rationalism apprenticeships are the first to go) the company's culture begins to wither, and the fresh new talent that might have enriched it is not being hired anymore, not even to start in the mail room – there *is* no mail room, there is no staff canteen, there is no family feeling, these things are beyond contempt.

The New Broom will not be in this business long, he will sell it up in three or four years and with his golden handshake move on to destroy another – sorry, rationalise another – big company, and what was once a happy, combative, loyal staff will meet only now and then, at the funerals of those who died in penury, or shot themselves in the workplace, or hanged themselves in gaol.

And this is good for the economy.

And it is *great* for the company.

Is it not?

Studies have shown that it isn't. The profits go up for two years, and they haemorrhage thereafter.

And there are reasons for this.

150

In the Australian Broadcasting Commission of 1967, for instance (of which a fair number of this readership will know little) there were unusefully employed in various apprentice, menial, underworked, superfluous or clerkly positions Michael Charlton, Mike Carlton, Richard Carleton, Bruce Beresford, Bruce Best, Peter Best, Paul Murphy, Maurice Murphy, Andrew Olle, Bob Connolly, John Hepworth, Bob Ellis, Bill Peach, Carl Schultz, Caroline Jones, Margaret Throsby, Pru Goward, Robyn Nevin, Ray Martin, Ray Alchin, Tony Morphett, Geraldine Doogue, Clive Robertson, Ted Robinson, Ted Roberts, John Tranter, Chris Masters, Kerry O'Brien, Geoff Barnes, Andy Lloyd-James, Jim Davern, Roger Hodgman, Allan

Ashbolt, Storry Walton, Gil Brealey, Gerald Middleton, Stewart Littlemore, Spike Milligan, Peter Luck, David Salter, Michael Pearce, George Negus, Bruce Petty, Graham Kerr (the Galloping Gourmet), Graham Kennedy, Peter Couchman, John Penlington, Bob Moore, Bob Carr, Peter Collins, Robyn Hughes, Robin Williams, the Oscar winner John Seale, the Oscar winner Dean Semler, the Oscar nominee Richard Francis Bruce, Robert Gibson, John Weiley, who directed Imax's *Antarctica*, John Duigan and – in the mail room – Ric Birch, director of the opening and closing ceremonies of the Olympic Games of 1992, 1996 and 2000.

These people have gone on to big and influential careers in the Australian and international media and films.

Had the ABC budget, in relative terms, been what it is now, five sixths of them would never have got a job in the media at all.

They would be driving buses, possibly, or teaching, probably, at TAFE or Bathurst College of the Arts, or pecking away at unfinished novels in gloomy retirement from other work, in garrets or garden sheds.

Or retrenched, or dead of suicide. Or chronically unemployed and drunk and boring. Or organising dud new religions.

What the ABC did then, you see – as the great Japanese corporations of recent decades did as a matter of course – was give its workers *room*, to vary their lives and their talents. They had tenure, and within the organisation varying possibilities, as reporters, directors, media personalities, war correspondents, publicity whiz-kids and officers in charge of humour, of religion, of worldly wisdom, of nocturnal reflection. And the fruits this bore, and the good it did Australia by providing at public expense a seedbed of talent for Australia's national profit has been immense.

That seedbed, however, is economically irrational and would now be dug up and paved and a carpark built above it.

A carpark is a much more rational investment.

Please name forty-eight of the ABC people of 1967 you would prefer never to have heard of.

Do it quickly. Expunge them.

The way a rationalist would.

Hurry up. Time is money.

151

Would it have been for the good of the country if these talents had not been found and encouraged, or would it have been for the bad of the country?

In their Orwellian way the rationalists have tried to silence such questions. Questions of right and wrong are impermissible now.

Right and wrong mean little to those who have no history, or humanity, or experience of ordinary work, and who put a lot of confected figures, a lot of noughts on the page, in their place.

Right and wrong and good and bad and even better and worse are not heard in the best editorial circles now.

'Historically inevitable' or 'economically unavoidable' or 'commendably efficient' or 'realistically competitive' or 'appropriately downsized' are in their place.

152

It's an American tendency, and it's been seen at different times in that country's history. The last time was in the Vietnam War when, finding the fiercest bombardment in human history was having little effect on a wily people with no defending air force, a strong culture, great patience and military ingenuity, and day by day and night by night they were losing the war on the ground, the Americans invented the Body Count in order to pretend they were winning it.

If we could show more bodies than they did, they reasoned, we were therefore winning the war. They cut off the body's ear and put it in a pile of ears to show how many they had killed.

Never mind that each body had seven or eight relatives, who grieved for him (or her), and planned to avenge him (or her). Never mind that he had, sometimes, a childless young wife who by local rules could never marry again. Never mind that the 'relocated' villagers became inflamed insurgents who joined the Vietcong and waited in jungle tracks to snipe you as you came into view.

You had a lot of bodies, and were, therefore, winning the war.

Never mind that you were killing people in their own country, in their own villages, in front of their own brothers and fathers and cousins.

The numbers showed you were winning the war.

'We're winning. Look at our pile of ears.'

Economic rationalists are pretty much like this.

Look at our trade figures. We're winning.

153

This American fondness for the numbers or, as they call it, the bottom line, is well illustrated in the way most nations now compute their economy.

If a company like BHP sacks two thousand workers (and incidentally wrecks a great city) and as a result the BHP share prices go up by fifty cents, this is regarded as a net gain for the company. If this in turn contributes to an improvement in the trade balance it is regarded as a net gain for Australia.

What has happened, however, *in human terms,* is that a few hundred very wealthy major shareholders have become even more wealthy while the lives of eight or ten thousand people have been devastated. They have only one life to live on this earth, and this could be the end of it.

When, likewise, Rupert Murdoch sacks four thousand of his employees worldwide and so himself becomes that year a hundred million dollars richer, this is regarded as not only a net gain for News Limited, but also a net gain and a victory for the economy, and thus the larger good.

Now, the idea that the rationalists here ask us to swallow is that Murdoch's personal wealth and happiness outweighs four thousand times the wealth and happiness of the four thousand lives he has so disordered, disrupted and wounded.

That when all the counting is done some people count, and *really* count, while others count not at all.

It is an idea familiar and widespread – in fascism, slavery, tyranny, empire, and Orwell's *Animal Farm.*

'All men are equal, but some are more equal than others.'

And all that matters in the end is the total, the numerical total. The trade balance. The current account. The human total is of no account.

Likewise the human deficit.

154

In a Budget speech by Australia's then Leader of the Opposition, Kim Beazley, in May 1998 – one written in part by the author – this idea of the human total versus the numerical total of statistics on a page was passionately aired.

'This is a surplus,' he said, 'that is built on a thousand small human deficits in ordinary lives.

'The shoes not bought. The teeth not fixed. The kids in backyard care, or the mother out of work. The apprenticeships not found. The annual holiday not taken because of the cost of a mother's nursing home. The birthday party cancelled. The family night out no longer affordable. The bicycle unrepaired and rusting. The university degree out of reach, and the fulfilling career therefore not had.

'The shame of the young school-leaver's hundredth

unsuccessful job interview. The corroding despair of the long-term jobless, and the alarm of their families. The grief of the parent farewelling a child who is leaving town for good.

'The factory closed. The trauma of selling up and moving. The hundred unspoken small goodbyes of ordinary people to their ordinary lives.

'These are the human losses, the human deficits, on which this accountant's surplus was built – by a government that has long ceased, or never learned, to care. The griefs and consolations, and the quiet unprotested sufferings which underpin the triumph of the Treasurer's numbers, and the failure of his decency.'

One man's surplus is another man's deficit, discuss.

155

'The nineteenth century carried to extravagant length,' wrote Maynard Keynes, 'the criterion of financial results as the test of the advisability of any course of action. The whole conduct of life was made into a sort of parody of an accountant's nightmare. Instead of using their vastly increased resources to build a wonder-city, they built slums; and they thought this right and advisable because slums "paid", whereas the wonder city would have been an act of foolish extravagance.

'We have to remain poor because it does not "pay" to be rich. We have to live in hovels, not because we cannot build palaces, but because we cannot "afford" them. The same rule of self-destructive financial calculation governs every walk of life. We destroy the beauty of the countryside because the unappropriated splendours of nature have no economic value. We are capable of shutting off the sun and the stars because they do not pay a dividend.'

156

There is economic gain, in short, and human loss.

There is company profit, and human loss.

And there is no such thing, in the end, as *savings*, in the absolute.

Only human loss, somewhere.

157

The inherent capitalist contradiction of profit out of evil and ill winds blowing nobody good has not gone unnoticed, however, or not always unnoticed. For across the First World, court cases have been mounted against cigarette companies for the knowing murder, carcinogenicide, of their customers; against silicone implant companies for the careless mutilation of their customers; against sexual harassers everywhere for bad behaviour in the office and wrongful dismissal; against the British government for improperly atomic bombing the homelands of Aborigines and poisoning them with radiation for the next half-million years; against the Australian government for the illegal annexation of a continent the size of Europe by the flimsy act of planting a flag on the equivalent of Dunkirk Beach, and murdering, kidnapping, raping and enslaving its owners for impertinently desiring to continue to live at peace in their homeland. Against the British government for continuing to countenance the manufacture of land mines, a policy which it has now abandoned. And so on.

And the economies of all these unheedful bodies have been disrupted by the upsurge of morality and lawful complaint against immorality in the international courts.

So economy follows morality *just* a little, discuss.

Economy and morality are kissing cousins, discuss.

158

During the writing of the last five chapters an apposite catastrophe occurred in the author's home suburb in the Northern Beaches of Sydney, Australia. A seaplane that does – or did – routine commuter flights and joy rides round the lovely adjacent waterways crashed into riverside bushland and killed all five people on board. The company that owned the seaplane had lost its licence two months ago because of suspect safety standards and then, remarkably, been given it *back* one month ago by the rationalist, cost-saving Howard government.

One of the former pilots, now working as a bus driver, had complained to the author's daughter four months before that all of the company's support staff had been sacked by the rationalists who had taken over the company, all of them inexperienced (of course) in flying, and so the mooring, cleaning and maintenance had to be done by the exhausted, overworked pilots.

The Howard government, moreover, had instituted a user-pays approach to air safety. If you were flying in cloud and wanted to learn if any other planes were flying in the same cloud – and if you were likely to collide with them – you had to *pay* to make the radio call.

And you were 'encouraged' by the rationalists in the company, your employers, not to do this.

And so the company profits were increased.

And so five people died.

And fifty or more adjacent lives were probably deeply wounded.

And so the company's licence was again suspended, and it will probably never trade again. And so the bureaucrats who, impelled by government policy, encouraged this rationalist practice (they called it in their Orwellian way Affordable Safety) will be brought to book and punished.

But not the academic theoreticians and corporate thinkers who with their fatheaded arithmetical dimness caused it all.

The blood of my neighbours, oh citizens, is on their hands, and cries out for redress.

This is a parable, a portrait in miniature, of what happens when only numbers are counted, and people discounted.

When the human factor is not put into the calculation.

There is company profit, and human loss.

They are hand in glove.

There is no alternative

It is not economically rational either, when you come to think of it, for the man behind the counter in the corner store to give you a new plastic bag each time he serves you. For you could use that plastic bag over and over.

'This is the one bag you're getting,' he should say to you. 'Bring it back and use it again. Do me a favour.'

That way he could save a whole lot of money.

He should give you only one plastic straw too.

'Wash it,' he should say, 'and use it over and over. When it splits I'll give you another. Do you think I am made of money?'

And that way he could sell you other goods a little more cheaply.

Customers, however, are curious entities, those who still have jobs and still spend money. They expect these little extras, like soap and towels and toilet paper and tea bags in hotel rooms, or they go somewhere else.

Our man may save on plastic bags and plastic straws, but he may lose customers. There is an *irrational* part of the economy then. A human factor.

Surprise, surprise.

The academic rationalists have not sufficiently studied the human factor, discuss.

160

Economic rationalists believe the economy and the people in it are entirely different things.

They believe the economy is an abstraction.

And not just people trading.

For in one of their more astonishing acts of careless neglect of this, the human factor, the economic rationalists have declared as a principle that the user should pay.

Like 'efficient and competitive' it's a phrase that sounds pretty good when you say it, but when you look into it you are horrified.

Because it means at its heart that Stuart Diver should pay for his rescue from under the rubble at Thredbo the three million dollars it cost the local services to get him out. He is the sole beneficiary of those local and state and commonwealth rescue services. So he should pay.

You might protest that he was the victim of an *accident,* but so are we all.

It is called life.

And parentage. And town. And country. And generation. And world movements of money. And the movement and multiplication of lethal viruses. The idea that you should pay, say, half a million dollars for the extraction of a brain cancer – because it's *your* brain cancer and that's what it cost the hospital to extract it – is a measure of how inhuman the idea is.

It's based on the premise that your cancer is your fault.

There are lots of things that are not your fault, or ours – earthquakes, depressions, plagues, jumbo jets that fall on the family home. And there used to be a method for dealing with these things.

And it worked too.

It was called government.

161

Government is a method of taking money out of your pocket and spending it on those things it thinks is necessary, and inviting your thanks or punishment at the ballot box after it has done so. From an average Australian wage it takes, for instance, twelve dollars a week for Medicare, the government health insurance system, seventeen dollars a week for primary education, sixteen dollars for secondary education, nine dollars for university education, nine dollars thirty for railways, five dollars ten for the paving and maintenance of public highways, one dollar for the ABC and ten dollars for the armed services. Though it all adds up to billions, the amount per day and per week it costs you is not very much – much less, for instance, than two days' parking in downtown Sydney – when you look at each individual service it provides in turn. Some of it you pay for twice, as when you buy a train ticket, or pay an entrance fee to university on the idiotic but widening principle that the user pays.

But it's not a bad system, government, and nothing like the creeping leukaemia that rationalists paint it as. It provides employment – in the Tax Office, in the water authorities, in the large bureaucracies that grow up around the politicians, their departmental offices and parliament buildings. It takes away a lot of tedious decisions from the individual, like whether or not he should himself repair the pothole in the road outside his home, or encourage his neighbour to do so, or set his own arm in plaster when it is broken. It clarifies and relaxes the citizen, and assures a lot of his future. And it gives him luxury items he could never otherwise, as a paying user, afford.

For the price per week of a can of Coca Cola, for instance, he gets the ABC. The ABC informs him pretty accurately of what the world is doing, makes him laugh and soothes him with fine classical music. It gives him a glimpse of world cinema and ballet and opera and much of the best of that fraction of good television drama that is in English, including high-class adaptations of the literary classics, and so on. It allows him to ring up and ask experts in many fields (gardening, animal recognition, suburban incest, company tax) their advice and intimate counselling. It gives him flood warnings and river heights and the coming weather and the birth dates of eminent people. And all for a dollar a week.

And the economic rationalists want it abolished.

It is not worth, they say, that dollar a week.

Better that dollar was spent on the can of Coca Cola.

162

Part of the reason for this, I think, is that it vividly shows, as a successful working government entity, just one of the many things that government can do much better than free enterprise, on a level playing field, in a global economy.

And the things that government can do are many and varied.

163

One of them occurred in 1994, when the Australian government ordered the exhuming of an unknown soldier and his reburial within the cenotaph in Canberra, the Australian capital. The then Prime Minister, Paul Keating, spoke by the grave, and it was very moving.

The author was there that day, and interestedly took note not only of the music and the old soldiers and the marching regiments of young soldiers approaching in sunlight along the road to Gundagai, but how it affected the local economy.

Flower sellers made money that day. Flag sellers. Tour-bus drivers. The hotels and motels of Canberra. The restaurants and hot-dog sellers. The video companies that recorded the ceremony and sold it through returned soldiers' clubs and retirement villages. The tourist authorities which, that day and long after, would have more customers come into Canberra and its environs because there was more reason to come now, to a new sacred site of the culture.

Money was made by lots of people. And a government decision made that possible.

And only a government could have.

164

Governments, likewise, organise the Olympic Games.

The Olympic Games is a startlingly successful method for a nation to publicise itself, and double or (as Barcelona did) quadruple its tourist potential for years, for decades, after the putting out of the flame. The Olympic Games empowers governments to spend money on railways, highways, hotel developments, theatre districts, sporting stadiums, brass bands, koala costumes, fireworks. It is an economic bonanza.

And only a government can organise it.

Economic rationalists, however, say that governments are always a drain on individual enterprise, and there should be fewer and fewer things that they do in the world. That business entrepreneurs can do what they do better and more efficiently.

That Christopher Skase, for instance, could do things better than Ben Chifley. Or Alan Bond than Franklin D. Roosevelt. Or Kerry Packer than Nelson Mandela. Howard Hughes than Mahatma Ghandi. Ted Turner than Lord Reith. Robert Maxwell than Yitzhak Rabin. Sam Goldwyn than Thomas Jefferson.

Make up your own list. And consider how well you would do in the thrall of such rulers.

Yet the economic rationalists say we need less of government, and more of them.

165

Governments, in fact, do a lot of things *more* efficiently than economic rationalists do.

Take insurance. When there are a lot of insurance companies competing equally on a level playing field in a global economy for the self-same customers there are a lot of supporting bureaucracies, investigators, troubleshooters, downsizers, investment advisers and tall, soft-spoken men who negotiate your claims down, way down.

These cost money. And the amount they cost has to be funded out of your insurance premiums.

If an insurance company loses customers – through, for instance, the badwill consequent on their brutal treatment of bushfire victims, as happened lately in Australia – your premiums go up, and go up again to pay for the advertising campaigns that rectify the deficit. And pay for the bigger and bigger wages of the executives, and the cost of their rotten investment decisions, and so on.

But . . . if all insurance was run by government,

and there was only one government insurance company, your premiums would be much cheaper.

For with only one bureaucracy there would be fewer wages to pay. There would be no money spent on advertising. There would be no *insurance salesmen.* There would be fewer arson investigations, the police would do it, and their word would be trusted. There would be no demeaning negotiation – as the author had – between the troubleshooters and the traumatised claimants to reduce the size of the payouts. The company would simply pay up.

And your premiums would be much less. Everyone would pay the same amount, and it would be paid, like Medicare, invisibly and fairly painlessly, as taxes.

And the government would have that much more money to invest, or spend on roads and schools and hospitals and cancer research and tourist initiatives.

But no, say the economic rationalists. Government must get out of the insurance business. And many governments did.

166

Governments have got out of a lot of businesses on the urging of the economic rationalists on their staffs and elsewhere. Out of airways and railways and electricity and water. Out of water transport and coal mining and hydroelectricity and gas pipelines. Out of telecommunications and post offices and dog-catching and steel manufacture and shipping and trucking and jobsearch and childcare and universities and colleges and also, amazingly, prisons.

And the world is a better place.

Pull the other one.

And the world is a cheaper place. And a safer place. And a happier place.

Give me a break.

167

After the privatising of British Telecom the phones of the inattentive were disconnected at the drop of a hat and it was harder, and it took weeks longer, to get a phone line repaired. After the privatising of water old women had their water cut off at an hour's notice and there was typhoid, suddenly, in Kent.

The privatised jobsearch utilities of Australia are charging *employers* four hundred dollars for their list of names of the unemployed. There are prison riots in privatised facilities in Victoria (fewer warders, less conversation, more annoyance and violence), rail lines are being closed and planes crashing. And bright kids from poor families are dropping out of the universities that might have saved them and turning, perhaps, to lives of crime, or suicide perhaps.

Under government this was not so. Or it was less so.

The economic rationalists therefore declare that what we need now is even less government.

And more of the above.

The above is the way the world is going.

There is no alternative.

168

It was summed up fairly well in 1975 by Frank Crean, then the Treasurer of Australia. 'With taxes,' he said, 'you buy civilisation.'

With private enterprise on a level playing field in a global economy, therefore, you buy chaos. And a lot of prettily worded evasions, like 'teething pains' and 'the hard yards' and 'the light at the end of the tunnel' and 'the recession we had to have' and 'a beautiful set of numbers' and 'turning the corner'.

There is no alternative.

169

There is *always* an alternative.

170

War, for instance.

Wars are fought to preserve a culture, to defend a way of life against a foreign power that would alter it. Young men are made to leave their homes and put their lives at risk under bullets and bombardment, in ships at sea or fighter-bombers in the air, because it is felt that a culture, a way of life, is worth preserving. Great amounts of money in hundreds of billions of dollars are spent on the arming, transport and housing of hundreds of thousands of young men organised in deadly peril to defend that way of life. And those who speak against that purpose, or act against that purpose, are tried as traitors and hanged or shot.

But . . . now, today, in the 1990s, when the invasion is *economic*, and the results of invasion just as tyrannous, dislocating, confusing and painful – though not, of course, as bloody – those who speak out *in favour* of the invasion, and collaborate with the invasion, those who used to be called the traitors, are given millions of dollars.

Apples, for instance, are no longer grown very much in Tasmania, an island once famous for them. Sugar is in crisis in Queensland, and bananas imminently at risk in New South Wales. The clothing trade is in its death throes in Victoria. The automobile industry in peril in South Australia. All over Australia piggeries are threatened by imported Canadian pork and bacon.

As in war, and as in a war that is lost, a way of life – no, many, many ways of life – are being strangled by invaders. And the Petains and Quislings and Lord Haw Haws who welcome the invaders are being hailed as great strategic thinkers, great intellects of the future, and paid hundreds of thousands in fees as consultants, and university professors, and company administrators.

It takes little intellect to surrender.

And no courage at all.

171

It is a surrender to global corporations of the taxes that buy our civilisation.

It is a surrender to foreign investors of money that, via government companies like Qantas, came back to us in federal budgets that funded our schools and hospitals and local kindergartens, and home care.

It is a surrender to foreign notions of necessary slavery, of the wage levels that define us, and the employment levels that define us, as a culture and a way of life.

It is becoming another sort of country because foreigners desire that it should be, and their agents, the economic rationalists, who abet their endeavours with propaganda.

It is a war we have *chosen* to lose.

172

We have been engaged in a kind of *passive totalitarianism.* An unwillingness to think about, or talk about, the things that matter most, trusting our leaders to think for us.

It is a far, far better thing that Australia import Arnott's Biscuits than it export Arnott's Biscuits, discuss.

It is a far, far better thing for Australians to pay money for Qantas tickets to foreigners than to Australians, discuss.

173

Can the outcome of this great war be altered? Can the current movement of history be turned around?

Well, possibly.

174

What is utterly certain across the world is that protectionism will return. It is *politically impermissible* for a world free market economy to continue to smash and mutilate the smaller countries. The governments that allow it will fall, and the political parties, however loopy, that oppose it will be elected, and will keep their campaign promises.

In Australia One Nation is already threatening to hold the balance of power, and Labor has vowed to protect sugar and reverse recent anti-tariff laws that hurt the recording industry, and the coalition government has delayed by five years the end of protection for the automotive industries.

The roll-back has begun.

175

May I make a modest proposal?

Let us ban, for three years only, all foreign camembert and mineral water. Let us ban these imports from Australia, and then, after three years, let them back in again.

What will happen if we do this?

Well, clearly, a lot more Tasmanian camembert (which is very good) will be bought and eaten, and a good deal more Taurina Spa and Deep Spring and Kyneton will likewise be bought and drunk. Farmers with natural springs on their land will begin to bottle the water and sell it. New brand loyalties will grow up.

And when the foreign brands return (with, perhaps, a tiny tariff on them) they will have competitors. And less Australian money will go to France and Italy via the sale of Perrier and Pellegrini.

Now, if we do this, will France and Italy cut off all trade with Australia in revenge? I doubt it. There is a good deal of history that argues otherwise. For they will get a good number of their Australian customers back after those three years, and that will be, if not ideal, acceptable.

They'll put up with it.

And so will the other countries whose industries we likewise target, for three years, or four years, while we preserve and encourage our industries at home. Sugar. Apples. Bananas. Red wine. Moccasins. Hats. Printing works. Toy koalas and kangaroos that are made now in Taiwan.

And, in the meantime, the whole house of winds and rumours will hopefully come tumbling down, and float away on the tide.

It will do this, probably, because of what happened in Indonesia.

176

Though profiting personally in billions, General Suharto ran a closed economy that made sense.

Its money's value was fixed by presidential decision, and it could not leave the country. Tourist dollars entered, but could not leave the country. The culture was rich – in sculpture, paintings, traditional dance, delicious, foul-smelling fruit and attractive homely architecture on green terraced hills – and, particularly in Bali, the arrival and departure of tourists enriched and did little harm to its inhabitants. The price of food was fixed by presidential decree.

General Suharto, however, had – rationally, quite rationally – been secreting billions of aid money and foreign investment in his family companies, colloquially known as Suharto Inc.

When the Asian currency meltdown hit there was no surplus cash to withstand it.

The IMF stepped in, and made its usual offer.

We will give you billions, it said, billions you must pay back, and in return you must 'free up' your currency, abolish price controls and wind back social services, and invite in, without let or hindrance, such foreign robber barons as wish to exploit your starving populace.

Miserably, Suharto did some of this.

The currency fell in value, and people suddenly could not afford food and began to starve.

Reacting predictably, they rioted in the streets, were shot dead by soldiers, and themselves burned and robbed the shops and houses of long resident and prospering Chinese.

The soldiers assisted in this persecution, and prior to murdering Chinese women would rape them serially, crying 'God is great!' in the moment of sexual climax. And afterwards, pleasured, cut their throats.

Finding these results unsuitable, Suharto refused to implement any further measures required by the rationalist screen jockeys of New York, who had never visited the country nor even slightly comprehended its multi-layered culture.

Suharto fell, and was replaced by Habibie, a grovelling acolyte of the General, who then evoked the dread name of Keynes to halt the massacre, starvation, loss of property, crisis in tourism, general puzzlement and murderous vengefulness that flowed from the IMF doing business in the usual way.

We must prop up our currency, said Habibie, and restore price controls and social services, and offer cheap tourist packages and, in Lord Keynes' phrase, prime the pump.

And so Indonesia, for the moment, was retrieved from chaos, carnage, and, apart from the loss of East Timor, political disintegration.

And so it was that the pallid gladiators of the IMF, by applying their usual numerology to distant specific events, caused – and directly caused – murder, rape, starvation, chaos, impoverishment, plague, civil war and similar benefits, the results they are famous for, among those with eyes to see.

But those with eyes to see, of course, do not include the governments of most of the western world, who are in the Cargo Cult, and with whitening knuckles hoping for the best.

These governments are falling one by one and shaking their fists and cursing, as they sink beneath the tide, the IMF and all its works.

177

And economic rationalism is suffering from a credibility problem, and not just because of Ralston Saul and this book and others, or its political fate in Britain, Australia, New Zealand, Canada, Russia and Eastern Europe.

It is because it is not working on the ground. Town by town and industry by industry, it is visibly not working. And everyone but the Grand Strategians can see it.

And the tattered, old name of Keynes is being summoned up as a cure for the damage it has caused.

178

Under Keynesian economics, the Australian federal government would buy up the Newcastle steelworks, rehire the sacked two thousand workers, make more and more steel with its outdated machinery, in its old-fashioned way, award Newcastle a submarine contract, and hope to sell the submarines to the many new emerging countries of a balkanised Indonesia.

It would invent, as Chifley once did, an Australian car, and market it, as Sweden's government did with its car, the Volvo, across the known world, and fund its federal budget with it. It would subsidise an acting school and theatre company in Dubbo, and another in Longreach, in Alice Springs and Kalgoorlie and Burnie, and allow their touring companies free tickets on Australian railways and airlines. It would buy up a million acres of western New South Wales and eastern South Australia to experiment with solar energy. It would massively fund research into cancer and AIDS in the hope of a breakthrough that would make us money – and, incidentally, increase human happiness. It would re-open the coal mines of the Hunter Valley, and pile up coal till there were international customers for it – in an independent Siberia, perhaps, or a newly democratic North Korea, where the winters are very cold, in Baffin Land or Tierra del Fuego. It would put a crippling tax on all Australian magazines printed overseas.

It would build an international airport in Parkes, and

a Very Fast Train from there to Sydney, and another from there to Darwin, and so help get goods cheaply overseas, and tourism to the far west, and population back to country towns. It would build an international airport outside Newcastle, with connecting Very Fast Trains and hovercrafts to Sydney. It would put big money into the Bowral Shakespeare Festival and bring to it big companies from both Stratfords and Russia and Japan. It would offer half-price airfares to first-time tourists to Australia. It would look at ways of reconstituting the inland sea.

It would go into debt to do this, in the traditional Keynesian pump-priming way, for tens of billions of dollars. To fund this debt it would put up taxes a bit, and tariffs a lot, to 1987 levels perhaps, to that medium level of trade viability before everything went to hell. It would ban from Australia altogether all crops picked by slaves and all goods built by slaves, according to a definition of slavery it would place before the United Nations and argue about. It would ban, as the world once did with South Africa, all products of tyranny.

And then it would wait for the world to respond.

It would do the usual Keynesian things, in short, just as the IMF, covering its eyes, has lately done to preserve Indonesia from civil war and chaos.

And wait for the world to respond.

And what would the world do then?

179

It would respond, I think, in the same way as it did when Australia swore it would not just keep its present greenhouse emission levels but put them up – with horror, bafflement, argument and then a weary shrug, and a wording of the eventual treaty that allowed Australia to do any fool thing it wanted.

For it's remarkable what our trading partners, and anyone's trading partners, will put up with in the end. The thousand percent inflation of Yeltsin's Russia. The thousand percent inflation of Begin's Israel. The child labour of Nepalese carpet factories. The feudal tyrants of Saudi Arabia who decapitate adulteresses. The firing squads and lethal injections of Texas. The fatwa against Rushdie. The harbouring by Spain of Christopher Skase. The holy wars against long-resident civilian populations by Netanyahu. The illegal slaughter in Australian waters of Australia's tuna by Japan 'for experimental purposes'. The amassment of foreign billions by Suharto's family. The hollow pretence at democracy by Marcos and Hun Sen. The detention and persecution of Burma's preferred Prime Minister Aung San Suu Kyi. The murder of Nigeria's preferred Prime Minister Moshood Abiola. The anti-Irish hit squads of Margaret Thatcher. The Howard Government's systematic denigration of the Aborigines. The murder of protesting students in Kent State University and Tianemen Square.

Is it likely, given this, that if we put a tariff back on bananas, and sugar, and moccasins, and camembert and Coca Cola, we will then be drummed out of the world community, never to return?

In the same way that America was drummed out of the world community for its unfair protective subsidisation of wheat? And Japan for the unfair protection of its rice?

That last sentence was a joke. And the one before.

But, as the man said, there are no jokes.

180

There is no great reason either why Australia's government should not buy back a controlling interest in Qantas, and the Commonwealth Bank and Arnott's and Akubra and Vegemite, paying the loans off slowly out of the profits of these proven companies – doing what the Attlee government did in 1946 when it renationalised coal and steel and De Havilland and Rolls-Royce. It's old-fashioned socialism of course, but its track record is better than anything that followed it.

181

It was old-fashioned socialism – a command economy – that ran and won World War II.

182

There are things, like insurance – especially health insurance – and Olympic Games and prisons and broadcasting and armies and navies that governments do better than anyone else. And there are things that they do just as well – and better, on the whole, than Robert Maxwell.

So whatever the tall, well-meaning Mark Latham says, there is no line of work that governments shouldn't be in, if it makes money and creates employment. None at all.

183

Mark Latham is what the Australian Labor Party has instead of a thinker. He wrote a book called *Civilising Global Capital*.

Fat chance.

184

It might have been more appropriately called *House-training the Crocodile*.

mercy. And family. And community. And continuity. And love. And home.

It is a bad thing. And, at its heart, corrupt.

It should be done away with.

It should be burned to the ground and its ashes sown with salt.

This I believe.

200

While I was writing these last chapters it was found that all of Sydney's water, the product of its twenty million taps, was undrinkable. It had two diseases, giardia and cryptosporidium, which the water inspectorate, a privatised concern, had not been asked to look for by the corporate utility that had been downsized.

The culture of the organisation, in short, had been eroded, as Ralston Saul observed of other corporations. The surviving officials were overworked and fearful and uncreative. No-one spoke up. The chairman of the company, lately an administrator of soccer, was not yet up to speed and hadn't been told there was a problem. And safety had been eroded, again, as it was in my local seaplane, by downsizing, cheaper options, efficiency and an almost existential haste.

Economic rationalism kills. It poisons. Criminalises. Traumatises. Hurts. Defies democracy. Offends all thoughts of civilisation. Is an enemy of

Prove that I lie

Hold onto that thought

on, but not substantially investing themselves – in things that in the end would bring back money to government and its dependants, also in billions. In fear of the *idea* of billions.

But . . . a billion is no longer all that much if you look at it closely.

A billion dollars Australian is the price of three thousand suburban houses, the price of all the houses in Greater Strathfield, say, which is large but not impossible to imagine; or the price of three jumbo jets or three submarines. It's one third of the yearly operating budget of the NRMA, one half of the annual budget of AMP. Three times the budget of *Titanic*, the movie, and only twice the cost, in modern terms, of *Titanic*, the ship. Or four times the total profits of *Crocodile Dundee*. It's imaginable. It's an amount that can be spent.

If it's politically too hard to raise and spend it, a government can easily do what the French did and move the decimal point to the left, so ten francs became one franc. And it worked.

We could do it too.

186

Imagine an Australia where the average price of the average house was thirty thousand dollars, not three hundred thousand. Or the price of a new car not

forty thousand dollars but four thousand. And the cinema ticket not fifteen dollars but a dollar fifty.

It might encourage people to spend money again. So people trade.

An economy exists because people trade, and not the other way around, discuss.

It's a fear of numbers that has the power of primitive superstition – like the number thirteen, or the year 1984, or eating fish on Friday – and it has to be dealt with.

187

A deeper cause might lie in the slow fading out of the world of the Christian religion.

In all its forms, the Christian religion convinced its European and Middle Eastern believers of a place that lay beyond death called heaven, or Beulah Land, or the Afterlife, in which virtue was rewarded by a happy, unceasing life among loved ones in a kind of green Arcadia. So time you spent on earth doing things for your fellow man was not time wasted. There was time at the other end of the contract, and time aplenty, to reap and enjoy the fruits of your labours.

As this belief in available immortality began to fade in the educated and warrior classes of modern Europe, and in the ordinary people puzzled by the

Holocaust, road accidents, cot deaths, leukaemia in children, famines in Africa and other distressing examples of divine unwisdom, a countervailing belief began to grow that time was valuable, and fleeting.

People started trying to pack more and more experience, and rewards, into the short time they had on earth.

This meant, in turn, that people were less inclined to spend a lifetime in one small business, passing it on to their children at death in the certain expectation of eternal life to come. They tended to diversify, sell up, reinvest, remarry, move on.

They tended to buy shares and bellow for big returns. They held out for golden handshakes, and calculated on skiing holidays in Gstaad, and (like the waterfront baron, Chris Corrigan) holiday homes in Tuscany.

The tendency to seek rewards now, now, was exacerbated by the loss of heaven and the Big Vacation to come.

A widespread twitchiness took over the world economy. An enormous, growing, existential tendency to hit and run.

A belief in the King Hit, the Knock-out Blow. In Crash Through or Crash.

Seed money was for damn fools.

Planted seeds took far too long to grow.

188

Hand in hand with this, and dependent on it, came a new definition of success. For success was earthly now. Success was no longer running successfully a small business and putting three kids through college and becoming an alderman on the municipal council. Success was now expressed in billions, like those of Murdoch, and world fame, like that of Michael Jackson, and global impact, like that of Bill Gates. Local eminence became, in the eighties and nineties, an insufficient outcome.

You had to have it all.

And the upshot of all this was the accelerated, asset-stripping, slash-and-burn and own-your-own-jet culture so well portrayed by Michael Douglas in *Wall Street.* Greed is good. Attack, devour and move on.

And the frenzied pumping of drugs into Olympic athletes, lest they fail in their first duty, that of Success.

And the rise of the political minder, and the policy-free campaigns of modern politicians by Saatchi and Saatchi and others.

The image above all. Watch out for Policy, it might lose you votes.

Success above all.

189

The steroid-swollen muscles of Olympic athletes are a parable of economic rationalism, discuss.

You eradicate the Olympic spirit, and all the honourable meaning of athletic effort, but you win the race.

And you make a lot of money. And then you are found out, and humiliated, and punished. And reviled as a fool for the rest of your days.

Follow the thread.

190

And with that ethic of success comes also a habit, if not quite an ethic, of lying.

Because to succeed you have to tell your customer that things will cost him less than they do, and so undercut your competitor. In the building trade this is almost universal: there is the stated cost, and then the actual cost – about eighteen percent more than the lie first told to secure the contract – and then the customer outrage, and the acrimony, and the court case, and the cost of the court case, and the time lost (often years) between the start of the building and its completion. The author sits in one such uncompleted building, five years later now. I call it home.

Sometimes it is worse than that, and the job completed on budget, and the workmen to save a few dollars are put in peril of their lives – and sometimes the customer too, as in any small provincial airline, anywhere in the world.

It's safety, sir, but it's *affordable* safety, or in other words danger; a lie whose effects can be fatal, as was the case in the bush above Berowra Waters.

For economic rationalism, and keep this in mind, can kill.

191

And so we have now the world we recognise, a world that so appalls old people who are now in their seventies and eighties, who remember another world. In which friendship meant something, and neighbourhood, and community, and nation, and party, and cause. And civilisation.

And charity, Princess Diana style, was not a foolish, outdated self-indulgence.

And people had value, and were not just replaceable units in a larger scheme of profit for the few.

And the human race in its old form was still with us, as you see it still in the west coast of Ireland, and the isles of Greece, and Western Samoa, and the small towns of New Zealand. And a smooth-talking,

conscienceless Beast was not yet subduing and eating up the world.

192

Let us look, at last, at the matter we must not think of, the subject we must not contemplate. Which is the nature of this Beast.

193

If it were what it said it was, a dedicated believer in efficiency, and the success that efficiency brings, it would do other than the things it does.

This is not, of course, to say it would think things through. It has shown itself in the past unable to do this, and in the present too.

It is to say it would behave in different ways.

Let me give you an example.

194

In England there is a privatised utility called Thames Water, once part of a great England-wide public service department that taxpayers owned outright, whose purpose is to bring water to the taps of London and Middlesex householders.

Its chairman, Sir Robert Clarke, is paid two hundred and thirty-three thousand pounds a year.

Now what is he paid two hundred and thirty three thousand pounds a year *for*? What enormous duties does he have? What great and onerous decisions does he have to make? What pressing policy initiatives to keep him awake at night?

Does he have to decide that water must be clean, and must come out of the pipe when the tap is turned? No, that happens already.

Does he have to outsell his rival water supplies? No, Thames Water is a monopoly. On a level playing field, of course, but a monopoly. The only player on the field.

Does he have to go to the government and face down their investigations? No, there are none of those – unless, of course, there is an outbreak of Plague. Does he work long hours? No, he presides over a monthly meeting, lasting half a day.

In what way, then, is he worthy of his hire, of two hundred and thirty-three thousand pounds a year? What, in an efficient and already downsized operation, justifies his pay? Anything you can think of?

Why, indeed, is he there at all?

195

Why, indeed, do we have this notion of the High Administrator, whose wage for a few hours' work

short, is the inefficient, uncompetitive, wasteful extravagant excess and self-indulgence of its profiteers, and their heirs and successors.

Prove that I lie.

198

Ergo, economic rationalism is a scam.

Like pyramid selling, it is not for you.

It is for your betters and their purpose of earthly pleasure.

You are part of that purpose, but you are expendable.

Expendable as Kleenex.

This is the matter of which we dare not speak, and now it is said.

199

And you, and the academics, and the corporation economists, and the editorial writers, and the middle managers, and the upper-middle managers, and the troubleshooters, and the minders, and the advertising men, and the Nobel judges, and the cabinet ministers, and the presidents and high court judges are all but feudal servitors of this purpose.

Prove that I lie.

This I believe

201

One thing more should perhaps be said, and it is this.

Economies vary, and are unpredictable and local and wayward, like the balls on a pool table thirteen cues down.

It was not predictable, for instance, that video hire and free-to-air television and unlawful videotaping off air and cable television and satellite television and club television and community-service television could co-exist, but they do. It was not predictable that live theatre would still be around sixty years after the coming of sound cinema, or forty years after television, or twenty years after colour television but it happened. It was not predictable that young boys by now would be spending so many hours indoors over computer games, fighting with non-existent alien invaders apocalyptic battles they are bound to lose. It was not predictable that dolls that wet themselves would have become popular with little girls. It was not predictable that Madonna, of all people, would accumulate fans, or the born-again Christian Bob Dylan lose them.

It was not predictable that the bipartisan concept of the welfare state, believed in equally by Attlee and Churchill (who was one of its creators) would be overthrown by a determined suburban female, Margaret Thatcher, and a senile Hollywood has-been, Ronald Reagan. It was not predictable that a resourceless, defeated, feudal-warrior culture, atomic-bombed and humiliated and colonised by hamburger-eating and baseball-playing barbarians, and universally detested by the civilised world in 1950 would in fifteen years be dominating the world. It was called Japan.

It was not predictable that the United States, which in 1986 had the biggest national deficit in human history, should by 1996 as an economy have outgunned Japan. It was not predictable that European communism would collapse overnight (what economist saw this coming?) or that Cuba would survive, impoverished but intact, ninety sea miles from America, its mightiest enemy, as a communist nation and a command economy, for thirty-eight years of beseiged, uneasy peace.

Nothing is that predictable, in short, and there are few rules that work for long.

And imagining, as economic rationalist theoreticians do, that one method of doing things can serve all situations is like saying that all families will *by definition* follow the classic Freudian model of father-murder and mother-incest. Some families do not have a father. Some are raised by a single grandmother, or a female couple who are lesbian. Some children are raised in orphanages, in prisons, in harems, on kibbutzes, in whorehouses, or by cannibals or wolves.

It is like saying that this golf game will be like the last one on this golf course. Or this pool game will be like the last one – against the same opponent, on the same table. Or tomorrow's weather will be the same as today's.

Things *vary*, and only a fool would behave as if they did not.

It is probable that a country like Australia, for instance, has problems that are unique. Like vast distances and a small population. It is entirely possible that the policy objective of a railway line which runs at a profit in such a place is unrealistic. And that a provincial airline which hopes to run at a profit will eventually be unsafe.

It is entirely probable that a government of such a country should run both services at a loss. It is probable that a country so large and dry needs a government that thinks more about water – its getting and cleansing and keeping – than other governments do. It is probable that a place like Tasmania, which has lots of water and few people, should have that water controlled by government and not by private enterprise. And so on.

It is likewise probable that a country as centrally placed and rich in cultural relics as Italy should concentrate its economy on tourism. It is probable that a country as ugly as South Korea should not. It is desirable the Galapagos Islands look after its wildlife, and Barbados look after its tall and marvellous cricketers, and Bali look after its temple dancers, and Fiji its firewalkers, and China its pandas, and Russia its abiding skills in medieval architecture and sculpture, and Holland its Van Gogh museum.

And Australia should do something with its desert sunlight. It has a lot of it.

And Telstra, on the cusp of a communications revolution, should not be sold off entirely. It might be making ten billion a year for its owner, the taxpayer, soon.

And Qantas, the world's safest airline, should be bought back while it is still the safest. It will surely, in the future, as climates alter and air travel grows more turbulent, make money.

Economies are local, and specific, and eccentric. And local needs, and local advantages, and local populations, should be looked to.

It stands to reason.

But not to economic rationalism.

202

The last word that should be uttered about economic rationalism, efficiency, competitiveness, downsizing and profit margin was uttered twenty-five hundred years ago, in an old Greek legend.

A farmer bought a goose, the story goes, and found to his surprise that it laid golden eggs.

The gold was genuine, and hugely valuable on the local market, and he made a lot of money.

His tastes improved and his needs grew more luxurious as the weeks went on. He began to run up bills.

The goose was not, he decided, laying the golden eggs fast enough.

He formed a plan.

He would kill the goose, and get all the eggs inside her all at once.

He did this, and found no eggs at all.

The goose needed time, and encouragement, and good and certain environmental conditions to provide the gold her master was so greedy for.

And the goose was dead.

And there were no more eggs.

Think on these things.

And follow the thread.